Advanc

Meaghan Dougherty's research is a compelling examination and critique of the transition experiences of social service workers in Canada. Her work is set against a backdrop of neoliberalism and meritocratic individualism, which values individual achievement and material success over an ethics of care and social justice. Theoretically informed, the stories of social service workers transitioning into work vividly highlight the power and performativity, the processes and struggles, of being and becoming a social service worker. As a social work educator and someone who has done narrative research, I highly recommend Dougherty's study into transition from education to work, and what this means for critical educators.

Dr David Hodgson, Senior Lecturer Social Work, Curtin School of Allied Healt, Faculty of Health Sciences

****

In *Need to Get Somewhere Fast: A critical examination of the transition from post-secondary education*, Meaghan Dougherty encourages us to question taken-for-granted assumptions about the relationship between school and work, and what it means to be "successful" within care-oriented disciplines. Dougherty brings to this work her scholarly expertise, as well as her professional wisdom as Child and Youth Care practitioner and educator at comprehensive community college. In her analysis of collaborative conversations with diverse new-to-career social service workers, she thinks with Foucault's notion of power, Judith Butler's concept of performativity, and posthuman ideas of becoming and entanglements, to critically examine their experiences as they navigate tensions between their values and neoliberal ideology. Dougherty complexifies common understanding about the transition from student to practitioner as a linear event to reveal a more relational, dynamic, and ongoing process. Although Dougherty's research is situated within the field of social services, her scholarship is relevant to all practitioners working in care-oriented professions within neoliberal institutions. She invites us to consider, "How can we work both within and against the structures that constitute and constrain us?" Dougherty's research creates openings for practitioners to reconsider what it means to become a social service worker, to live a good life, and to imagine more just and equitable futures. Simply put, *Need to Get Somewhere Fast* is brilliant, engaging, and accessible, and makes a significant contribution to the field of practitioner education.

—**Cher Hill**, PhD, Teacher-Educator

****

It is no easy task to break through the linear construction of just about every journey, be that the journey from childhood to adulthood, from man to woman, or, as in this book, from student to practitioner. Yet this book manages not merely to critique this linear construction of the student-practitioner transition, but it also serves to validate the value and meaning of the uncertainties that come with journeys in which we never quite arrive anywhere in particular. In a brilliant discussion of the concept of transition, Dougherty weaves in complex ideas of becoming and entanglements, as well as feminist theories of performativity, and brings to life the very real reflections, doubts, and confirmations of five social service workers. The text creates endless space for the voices of the workers to shape the narrative, to build new theoretical insight, and in so doing, to demonstrate that co-creation of knowledge between researcher and participants is itself an act of social justice that disrupts the often invisible coercion of neoliberal determinism. This is a short, very concise book that will appeal to the practitioner as much as it will be a delight for the theoretician!

—**Kiaras Gharabaghi**, PhD, Dean, Faculty of Community Services, Toronto Metropolitan University

****

A unique and insightful perspective on the concept of transition from school to social service work. Filled with experiences and stories of social service workers, this book aims to guide individuals in viewing the transitional process as an ongoing, individualistic, and self-empowering one. Need to Get Somewhere Fast should captivate readers navigating their place in the demanding yet rewarding nature of social service work.

—**Simran Notra**, Addictions Counsellor

****

As someone who entered school with the goal to be seen as a professional and have my name on an office door; Meaghan Dougherty's book looks at how one actually defines success. The interviews she conducts show a common theme of feeling like you need a piece of paper to prove your worth within the field of social services. There is no one ideal of a social services worker and anyone getting in the field should read this book if you want to feel less alone as you transition from school to the working world.

—**Keshia Cleaver**, BA Child and Youth Care

Need to Get Somewhere Fast

A critical examination of the transition from
post-secondary education to work

Meaghan Dougherty

ISBN 978-1-64504-256-3 (Paperback)

ISBN 978-1-64504-257-0 (Hardback)

ISBN 978-1-64504-258-7 (E-Book)

Library of Congress Control Number:

Printed on acid-free paper

This book is part of *Critical Practitioner-Scholars*

Series Editor: Barry Down and Robert Hattam

Dedication

This work is dedicated to everyone who fights to remake the world anew.

Table of Contents

Preface   xi

Foreword   1

Part 1: Understanding Transition   5

Chapter 1   7
Why is the School to Work Transition Important?

Chapter 2   21
The Purpose of Education and its Relationship to Work

Part 2: Transitioning to Social Service Work   39

Chapter 3   41
Who are Social Service Workers?

Chapter 4   53
"I Should be Further Ahead"—Power Relations in
Transition

Chapter 5   75
"Never Enough"—Performing as Social Service Worker

Part 3: Re-Imagining Transition   101

Chapter 6   103
"We are Constantly Transitioning"—Transition as
Becoming

Chapter 7   121
Risks and Responsibilities

Appendix A: Methodological Approach   135

Preface

When I open a new book—and yes, I am still committed to the print version of books—I always begin with the preface. I want to hear from the author about who they are, why they engaged in the work, how the book came to be, and what the author intends the work to do. I hope to provide you, the reader, with a peek behind the curtain of the purpose and process of creating this book.

Who?

I am an educator who teaches in a comprehensive community college in an applied program for students who intend to work with children, youth, and families who face multiple vulnerabilities. I came to that role through my own experience as a practitioner and a leader in social services. Through my experiences doing the work, I thought that I knew what students needed to learn to be effective social service workers. I truly believed that I could provide the information students needed; they would internalize that information and then apply it in their relational work. My dissertation research began with an intention to identify curriculum gaps to ensure students could seamlessly apply their learning from post-secondary to the field. As

I began learning about education, I recognized the simplicity and ignorance in my initial intention. Through my studies and research, I started to examine the relationship between education and work, the role of schooling, and the relational processes of teaching and learning. For me, this led to questions about how students transition from their educational experience to working in the field and what tensions might arise as students apply their learning in practice. In social services and in other fields, these questions can have significant implications on the lived experience of the students/social service workers and on those they serve (commonly referred to as 'clients').

What?

This book is divided into three parts to explore key questions about transition. Part One critically explores the transition from post-secondary education to work. I examine the relationship between education and work, and seek to complexify the dominant view of the transition from post-secondary education to work as a linear, distinct event that can be assessed through primarily financial indicators. Complexifying our understanding of transition as critical scholars/educators and critical practitioners allows us to move beyond deficit-focused interventions and offers a more comprehensive understanding of how factors beyond the individual student constitute and constrain the transition experience.

This work is grounded in the narratives of social service workers. Part Two focuses on how social service workers are defined in this work. I also examine how social service workers, practitioners who work with marginalized people in community-based, not-for-profit agencies, are a liminal group who face significant challenges, including tenuous work, vicarious trauma, and precarity. I introduce the participants who shared their experiences in this inquiry and my approach to relating to their narratives. I critically analyze the participant narratives. These narratives of navigating the neoliberal institutions of school and work highlight power relations, idealized expectations, and the experience of transition as an ongoing process. Their narratives illustrate the importance of resistance, criticality, and exploring alternate discourses of what it means to successfully transition into a professional role.

In Part Three, I put more-than-human, relational, and performative ontologies to work to see what is possible, from a practical, ethical perspective, for educators and educational institutions.

Drawing on the experiences of social service workers navigating the transition from school to work promotes a new imagining of the phenomenon of transition. This new imagining has meaningful, ethical implications for educators and educational institutions in supporting students with their transition to work. It also promotes a better understanding of the transition process for current and future students. With a more complex understanding of transition, post-secondary educators, students, employers, and researchers can consider the pressures on students to "get somewhere fast" and support transition processes that involve complex and interrelated factors.

Why?

I hope this book helps illuminate the complexity of the post-secondary education to work transition, encouraging educators to critique the neoliberal promises of education leading to employability and a good life and examine their own role in reproducing these promises. This includes examining educational practices and curriculum and questioning how education can help prepare students for the transition process. Educators will better understand the nuance of the transition experience and be better equipped to support students moving into the workforce. Post-secondary educators teaching in disciplines related to helping professions and social service work (e.g., Child and Youth Care, Social Work, Human Services, Humanities and Social Sciences) will be familiar with the tensions between teaching/learning and preparing suitable workers. I hope that reading this book catalyzes educators to deconstruct dominant ideas of success and explore students' conceptualizations of a meaningful life. Educators in applied programs may find the exploration of the tensions between education and employment helpful to how they navigate and support student practicum experiences and internships, balancing theory/practice and learning/employability. In addition to educators, this book can be relevant, meaningful, and generative for post-secondary students, who may see their own challenges and pressure to get somewhere fast represented in the analysis. The experiences offered by the social service workers will be useful for students studying in helping disciplines and interested in social service work. The narratives of the social service workers encourage students to question the expectations they have of themselves and are experiencing from others, in relation to their transition from school to work. The book asks students to pause and consider alternate discourses that may be helpful to them in navigating school and work. I also encourage social service practitioners to reflect on their own transition process and examine how the taken-for-granted ideas of success promoted in school and work influence their practice. Social service practitioners will recognize the tensions involved in relational practice and the discourses that constrain them; understanding these constraints allows social service practitioners to resist in ways that are meaningful and improve the material conditions of the lives of others. Administrators in social services and funding agents would also benefit from better understanding the experiences of their employees, balancing relational practice and providing performativity measures to justify their work.

How?

The process behind this book is one of serendipity. I was very lucky to have Barry Down serve on my dissertation committee. After reviewing my dissertation research[1], he thought my inquiry might fit within his series on the Critical Scholar-Practitioner. I am filled with gratitude for Barry and for this opportunity with DIO Press. There are a number of other people without whom this book would not have come to be.

First and foremost, I am grateful to the participants who shared their time, experiences, and narratives with me. I learned, and continue to learn, so much from our intra-actions. I hope I have honoured your stories. I am also so thankful to Becky Cox, Suzanne Smythe, and Michael Ling, who encouraged, supported, and pushed my thinking in ways I did not know was possible during my research process. I truly appreciate the ongoing support that Becky has provided, throughout this and every other academic process I have engaged in. Your advice, humour, and encouragement mean more than you will ever know! Thank you to Gillian Judson, Patt McGuire, Joe Dougherty, Isa Purcell, Michael Chahal, and Gary Tennant for reading and providing invaluable feedback throughout my writing process. And a huge thank you to my writing group friends—Kristy, Jacky, and Kari. You make writing a relational process. I also want to thank my husband, Rob, our dog, Sunny, and my family—Patti, Joey, Jenn, Jesse, Kim, Emily, Alex, Caitlin, Caden, and Jasper for always being there!

Through my relations with these people and others, I continue to learn and grow. I want to emphasize that my thinking about transition, power, performativity, and becoming continues. I draw on the narratives and my relational encounters with the participants regularly. Those intra-actions continue

---

1   This book is based on my dissertation research (Dougherty, 2019) and I have explored some of the ideas discussed here in other publications (Dougherty, 2021; Dougherty, 2022).

to shape my thinking/doing/being. This research is agential in my becoming-researcher, becoming-educator and becoming-human. I hope it engages your thinking in generative ways.

Foreword

When I began teaching in schools thirty-five years ago, I became interested in how power functions to constitute individual identities and imagined futures. As a novice teacher, I wondered (and still do) why some students thrived and others fell by the wayside. As a working-class kid myself, I bought into the belief that education was the holy grail to finding a secure, well-paid, white-collar job. It became the yardstick for measuring one's success based on individual merit, ability and effort. Family and teachers alike reinforced the belief that if you study hard and obey the rules, then success will follow. Back then, the idea of a smooth school-to-work transition seemed to be relatively straightforward and certain. The story went something like this. Some kids were deemed to be smarter than others and, therefore, more deserving. The smarter kids headed off to university if their parents could afford it and eventually high-paying and rewarding careers. Because of their intellectual inferiority, the others were cajoled into vocational pathways where they were prepared for low-status manual jobs. This bifurcation between academic and non-academic students was justified and sustained by the ideology of meritocracy, and the impartiality of schools in determining the labour market fates of young people and, like most beliefs, seems immutable.

Moving to the 21st century, the circumstances are radically different, although the narrative is eerily familiar. The profound changes wrought by global capitalism and the forces of neoliberalism have unleashed a range of authoritarian and anti-democratic policies on schools and those who inhabit them. Schools have been ruthlessly absorbed into the orbit of capitalism characterized by escalating levels of commodification, vocationalization, precarity, individualism, competition, inequality, poverty, racism, environmental damage, violence and war. This can easily lead to a sense of fatalism and determinism about how things are.

At this historical moment, society faces an existential crisis that demands action. In the tradition of Paulo Freire, educators have a responsibility to fight against fatalistic discourses and, instead, must work toward creating alternative possibilities. At the heart of this wider democratic project is a commitment to the struggle for social justice. This involves seeing the world from the point of view of strangers and walking in their shoes. This is exactly what this book sets out to achieve. In the process, it begins to breathe new life into the question of what it means to be educated and more fully human.

This is why this book is so welcome. Meaghan Dougherty has sought to interrupt the logic of neoliberalism and its dehumanizing impact on education and the world of work. She challenges narrowly conceived and instrumentalist versions of school-to-work transitions and the preoccupation with measurement, standardization, competency-based training, compliance and self-interest. As a counter to these mega narratives, this book documents the lives of five social service workers in the Lower Mainland of British Columbia to investigate how they navigate the complexity of their work with some of the most marginalized groups in society. Based on these stories, the book interrupts hegemonic discourses of individualism, commodification, performativity and deficit thinking, and shifts the focus to intentions, relationships, morality and social action based on the values of compassion, social justice and solidarity.

In providing up close, thoughtful and theoretically informed attention to the lives of practitioners in the field, Meaghan Dougherty adds rich insight into the tensions, dilemmas and conflicts social service workers encounter daily as they deal with trauma, poverty, addiction, mental health concerns, histories of violence, developmental delays and homelessness. This kind of critical intellectual (and emotional) work allows us to move outside dominant ways of seeing the world and begin to imagine what might be. Meaghan Dougherty has produced a deeply instructive book about what it means to be a critical-practitioner scholar and one that anyone concerned with this cultural work will benefit from and enjoy reading. In closing, I will leave you with Meaghan Dougherty's heartfelt words because they are a source of inspiration and an invitation to join the struggle for a better world.

> *I believe I have, as an educator and as a citizen, a responsibility to think and act in ways that allow for different potentialities. I have an ethical responsibility and a response-ability (i.e., in an ability to respond) (Barad, 2012) to make things more equitable and just for students, workers, and all human and non-human citizens of the world.*

Barry Down
Perth, December 2021

Part 1

Understanding Transition

Chapter 1

Why is the School to Work Transition Important?

There is a widely-held belief in North America about the relationship between school and work. It takes various forms but generally goes something like this—young people need to work hard and achieve good grades in secondary school to be accepted into a 'good' college or university. Once in post-secondary, students need to work even harder to differentiate themselves from the masses to obtain a 'good' job. Achieving a 'good' job depends on one's effort and work ethic and is necessary for living a 'good' life. Being successful means navigating the pathway from school to work appropriately and, ultimately, obtaining a job that financially supports the desired lifestyle. In this story, consistent with our hypercapitalist society, success is synonymous with financial wealth.

In this narrative about the relationship between school, work, and ultimately, living a good life, education is portrayed as a ladder of opportunity. Through their own hard work and dedication, people navigating oppression, poverty, racism, trauma, and other systemic barriers can improve their social standing. Education allows for social mobility; inequity can be addressed through intergenerational improvements in one's social class, such that one's class origin no longer predicts their destination (Brown, 2013). This story is known as the

American Dream, although its reach extends far beyond the borders of the United States. This story is riveting, appealing to our sense of autonomy and self-empowerment and while it is not entirely false, it is not the whole story. The relationship between school, work, and living a good life is nuanced and complex. The complexity of this relationship remains largely unexamined by the general public, and this lack of critical examination impacts students, workers, education, perspectives on work, and understandings of what it means to live a good life. This book aims to begin to examine some of the assumptions embedded in the story of education as a pathway to success, critically explore the relationship between school and work, and imagine what might change if the *transition* was understood differently.

In order to understand the transition from school to work differently, we first need to examine how it is currently conceptualized. In this chapter, I explain how education, specifically post-secondary education, is increasingly viewed as an arm of industry; vocationalized education tailors learning to specific jobs or careers to improve the employability of students (Grubb & Lazerson, 2004). Education is the pathway to employment. The transition from post-secondary education to work is significant for the individual and society. Due to the significance of this transition, educational institutions attempt to increase successful transition for the good of the student and society more broadly. However, deficit-focused interventions reproduce inequity by placing responsibility for transition on the student without critically examining the structural constraints of the labour market.

Simply put, interventions focus on the supply-side of the transition, socializing students to be more employable without recognizing job market realities that limit employability. This provides the foundation for questioning the dominant story of education, work, and success. I introduce that the transition experience of social service workers—a liminal group that engages in front-line work with marginalized people—helps demonstrate the complexity of transition and offers new imaginings for critical practitioner-scholars in social service work and education.

Education has become increasingly vocationalized, such that all levels of education serve to prepare students for work in a specific occupation or career (Grubb & Lazerson, 2004). As education becomes increasingly vocationalized, occupations become increasingly professionalized, such that unique specializations emerge (e.g., paraprofessional positions like paralegal, dental assistant, imagining technician, human resources), and specific credentials are required for positions that did not previously require an education (e.g., warehouse technician, medical office assistant). In this cycle, education and work reinforce one another and justify the growth and necessity of the other. As discussed in more detail in Chapter 2, the purpose of education becomes entangled with employment, and students attempt to navigate their education to obtain the credential that will enable their desired career.

This dominant understanding of schooling, work, and 'success', implicitly accepted by the general public, is also the foundation for much of the educational research on transition. In this literature, transition is touted as a critical point for the individual and for society. Transition is a distinct phase between education and work that can be assessed as successful or unsuccessful using pre-determined outcomes like employment and/or income. Transition may be deemed successful, within this perspective, when a student completes a credential and transitions into employment that is commensurate with that credential. Although school-to-work transitions can happen at any point—including from secondary school, trade schools, vocational training, or other job training programs—the focus of this book is the transition from post-secondary education to work. Post-secondary education is portrayed as the pathway to a highly skilled and globally competitive workforce and as the pathway to individual financial success. Note how, for example, post-secondary education is promoted as the best route to a quality job in this Statistics Canada report on the labour market outcomes of graduates in Canada:

> Knowledge and skills are increasingly important to innovation, productivity, economic growth and competitiveness. For Canada, a better-educated population and a highly skilled workforce are vital to ensure successes in the face of growing global competition. Higher education can provide individuals with knowledge and skills needed to participate in a changing economy and society. As jobs become increasingly knowledge-intensive, having a postsecondary credential is the best route to a well-paying, quality job in Canada. (Ferguson & Wang, 2014, p. 4)

Successfully transitioning from post-secondary, with a credential, to employment promotes the overall success of the student and the development of an educated and skilled workforce that allows Canada to compete globally.

Individual and Societal Significance of 'Successful' Transition

This focus on the individual and societal importance of school-to-work transition shapes existing educational research. Individually, an unsuccessful transition is associated with unemployment, under-employment, or precarious work. Societally, unsuccessful transition means the lack of an educated and employed public, which, according to human capital theory, results in being less competitive globally (see Brown et al., 2001). Due to the significance of transition, areas of research examine young people who are not employed, in education, or training to determine ways to protect students from unsuccessful transitions, which can result in unemployment, social exclusion, substance use, and various mental health concerns (Bäckman & Nilsson, 2016).

Given the potential negative consequences of an unsuccessful transition, educational research often focuses on the barriers to successful transition for various populations of students to derive evidence of effective interventions for improving transition. Interventions may include career development programs (e.g., Koen et al., 2012) or mentorship and apprenticeship models (e.g., Renn et al., 2014; Lang, 2010; Ogbuanya & Chukwuedo, 2017). Some researchers use statistical analyses to examine the personal characteristics (including psychological traits, family structure, socio-economic status, etc.) of students who have transitioned to work to determine the predictors of more positive or negative transition experiences (e.g., Yang et al., 2017; Pinquart et al., 2003). Other research focuses on student goals and aspirations in relation to their transition, and how these relate to their values, identity, and fit with later employment (e.g., Vuolo et al., 2012). This literature demonstrates that transition outcomes can be influenced by a student's personal characteristics, goals, and aspirations, and the degree of support available to the student.

Although this research takes varied approaches to assess transition, the theoretical understanding underpinning this body of literature is that transition is a linear process that can be assessed as 'successful' or 'unsuccessful'. In most educational research, having a 'successful' transition assumes the completion of post-secondary education and subsequent employment commensurate to the student's educational credentials; this can be assessed in terms of income. This definition of a 'successful' transition needs further examination in two areas. First, is the assumed trajectory from school to work realistic for all students? What does the transition look like for students who study and work simultaneously? Or return to school after working in the field? How can these varied trajectories be adequately explored using current conceptualizations of transition as a distinct stage existing between school and work (see Ashton & Ashton, 2016)? Second, is income an accurate measure to assess 'success'? How does this account for students who transition into fields that are not well-paid? How is transition assessed when students are motivated by factors that are not purely financial? What does transition mean in care-oriented disciplines, like social service work? How do students in these disciplines navigate financial-oriented definitions of success, and how do they reinscribe their own definitions of success? This book explores some of these questions to better understand transition in a broader context, and to complexify current narratives that emphasize student responsibility for transition.

Maximizing 'Successful' Transition through Deficit-Focused Interventions

The hegemonic story of education as a pathway to success—individually and for our nation—is built upon understanding the transition from school to work as a linear progression that can be assessed through financial indicators like income. Interventions are designed to maximize 'successful' transition experiences. This intervention-focused approach emphasizes student deficit and individual responsibility for transition. Focusing on educational interventions to promote 'successful' transition places responsibility for transition on the individual student; from a deficit perspective, the student needs additional supports from the institution to compete for employment. This focus emphasizes the student's responsibility to commodify themselves as a marketable "bundle of skills" to sell their labour (Urciuoli, 2008, p. 211). Commodification promotes skills as discrete units of knowledge that one obtains through education and holds in relation to productive job performance; these skills involve internalizing ideals of a disciplined worker, including being self-directed, self-improving, and competing for social mobility (Urciuoli, 2008).

Some of the transition literature mentioned above examines how students vary in their capacity to effectively commodify themselves based on individual, family, and social characteristics (e.g., Yang et al., 2017; Pinquart et al., 2003). More privileged students can mobilize their social (e.g., professional networks and connections) and personal capital (e.g., internships, volunteer, and work experience) to aid in job search and obtaining employment, thus demonstrating a more 'successful' transition (Lehmann, 2019). Compared to their counterparts from more privileged backgrounds, working-class students rely primarily on human capital (i.e., educational credentials) to obtain employment (Lehmann, 2019). Working-class students often engage in additional post-secondary education (with work placements) to improve employability as they do not have family connections or professional networks, access to exclusive internship opportunities, or the financial ability to engage in unpaid work (Lehmann, 2019). Without examining these social inequities, interventions often focus on correcting deficits in individual students by building social and personal capital and encouraging students to internalize neoliberal expectations of the ideal worker. This could include dressing and communicating in a professional manner, demonstrating deference for the employer, and having a positive, can-do attitude (see Valadez, 2000). For example, interventions in career development and job-placement programs socialize students into a more "professionalized identity"—one that is racialized, classed, and gendered—rather than providing new knowledge, skills, or understanding (Hull, 1993; Valadez, 2000). These interventions emphasize personal responsibility in the need to work hard and project a positive and professional image while failing to account for labour market reality, societal constraints, inequity and other obstacles faced by the students transitioning into the workforce.

While this focus on student interventions is contextualized as promoting equality and enabling students to compete for 'good' jobs, this approach reproduces inequities and reinforces the concept of the 'ideal worker'. As noted, these interventions often reinforce a classed, raced and gendered 'professional' and fail to recognize the complexity of school-to-work transition beyond the individual student's responsibility. That is, these interventions may focus on assimilating and commodifying students to be attractive to employers without examining labour market realities that influence employment. In focusing on interventions for students, educational institutions emphasize the supply-side of the school-to-work transition, neglecting to critically examine the workforce, including the types of jobs available and what makes for 'good' or democratized work (Kincheloe, 1995).

Who Am I to do this Work?

It is important to note that I began this project fully embedded in the dominant discourses of school, work, and transition. Many years before the research that is the topic of this book, I had navigated my own experience through post-secondary education and into working in social services. I went to university intending to get a good job. I wanted my classes to be relevant and responsive to labour market needs so I would be well-equipped and ready for work. After achieving my credential and moving into employment, when my work was tenuous—due to contract work, loss of funding, or lay-offs—I saw moving from position to position as a personal deficit. I wondered what I was doing wrong and how I could enhance my resume to better sell myself. When, many years later, I moved into a faculty position, teaching students who will work in social services, I saw my past self mirrored in my students. I saw students, consumed with grades, credentials, and resume-enhancing experiences, under considerable pressure to position themselves for a successful transition to working in social services.

As an educator, I wanted to determine how I could teach people to be better social service workers. What did they need to know to be more effective in their role? With my experience working in social services, I knew the challenges those served by social service workers face. My ethical imperative, both as a social service practitioner and as an educator of future social service workers, was to improve the lives of those receiving service (i.e., 'clients'). I thought creating more effective social service workers would ultimately promote more positive change for those served by social services. The intention was good, but we know that the road to hell is paved with good intentions. I had a simplistic view of the relationship between education and work, and my role as an educator in preparing students to transition to work. Had I rushed to possible interventions to increase practitioner efficacy without deconstructing my assumptions about school, work and transition, I would have reinforced dominant conceptualizations of transition and reproduced a student-deficit approach. Rather than assume the students are lacking, and determining what they need to be more effective, I listened to their experiences navigating school and work. I heard about ongoing tensions and challenges and how they made sense of their role as social service workers.

Through my research, I came to critically examine my own assumptions about school and work, but also what it means to do meaningful work and how that relates to living a good life. Inspired by critical theorists who question dominant understandings of education as a meritocracy that promotes social mobility, I explore the purpose of education and labour market realities to better contextualize the participants' experiences as shared in their narratives. As an educator and as a citizen, I believe I have a responsibility to think and act in ways that allow for different potentialities. I have an ethical responsibility and a response-ability (i.e., in an ability to respond) (Barad, 2012) to make things more equitable and just for students, workers and all human and non-human citizens of the world. To engage ethically with this work, I need to deconstruct common assumptions of how things are; these taken-for-granted beliefs further entrench inequity and dismiss the differential constraints experienced by people as inevitable.

Complexifying Conceptualizations of School to Work Transition

In keeping with literature that questions the simplistic relationship between education and work, this book interrogates the story that hard work leads to a good life. Specifically, I contextualize investigations of the school-to-work transition within broader social, historical, economic, and institutional narratives that influence this process. I do this by exploring how social service workers in the Lower Mainland of British Columbia navigate their transition from post-secondary education to work. Drawing on critical narrative inquiry, I co-constructed narratives with five social service workers over a series of interviews (a more comprehensive explanation of the methodology is available in Appendix A). Social service workers, as discussed in greater detail in Chapter 3, work in front-line positions in community-based not-for-profit agencies. As such, they work directly with marginalized people who face increasingly complex challenges such as trauma, poverty, addiction, mental health concerns, histories of violence, developmental delays and homelessness. This challenging and precarious relational work often goes unrecognized in society and does not lend itself well to traditional conceptualizations of 'success'. That is, social service workers may have different understandings of what a 'good' job is and what it means to be 'successful'. As social service workers engage from an ethics of care, their experiences navigating school and work can provide an alternative perspective on transition.

Exploring how social service workers navigate transition and what they 'bump up against' (Clandinin, 2013) through that process helps illuminate taken-for-granted ideas of school, work, and success. Specifically, through these transition experiences, tensions regarding the purpose of education, what a 'good' job is, what it means to do your job well, and how meaningful work contributes to living a good life are highlighted. These questions and others, have important implications for educators, students, and critical social service practitioners. Examining transition differently may help educators question their role and purpose. Are educators training students to be good workers? Are educators emphasizing critical exploration and learning? How are educators reproducing and/or resisting the narrative that education is the pathway to success within their educational institutions? How do educators recognize inequities in their classrooms? What critical examinations of school, work, and what it means to live a good life are happening? How might educators think about teaching and learning differently? Raising these questions with students can help them engage critically with discourses that constitute and constrain them, allowing them to recognize and resist neoliberal ideas of work and success. Social service practitioners may help reshape current definitions of 'success', focusing on the relational work they do with others and how that work can improve the material conditions of the people they serve. Their experiences raise important questions about what constitutes meaningful work and how the organization of work influences one's sense of purpose and connection.

Those who shared their transition experiences with me expressed, in different ways, the pressure they felt in their transition, this *Need to Get Somewhere Fast*. The participants weren't clear on where they were trying to get to, or how to get there, but they knew they needed to get there quickly to be viewed as a success. This book attempts to slow things down to fully explore what contributes to this pressure and understand how reconceptualizing transition shifts the focus away from student deficit and individual responsibility.

This book is organized into three parts. The first part examines common understandings of school, work, and transition and works to deconstruct a simplistic explanation of this relationship. Specifically, this section critiques the individual responsibility placed on students to actualize the promise that post-secondary credentialing leads to commensurate work and a good life. The second part focuses on the social service workers who shared their transition experiences and the themes that emerged from their narratives; specifically, how power influences their transition, how they perform their role as social service workers, and how they experience transition as an ongoing process. The analysis of these themes allows for transition to be re-imagined in Part Three. I examine the risks and potential rewards of reframing transition for students, social service workers, teaching and learning, educators, education, and work. I explore the responsibilities of educators and of practitioners in shaping how students experience school, work, and transition. Together, this can help write a new story about the purpose of education, democratized work and ultimately, what it means to live a good life.

References

Ashton, H. S., & Ashton, D. N. (2019). "Bring on the dancers": Reconceptualising the transition from school to work. *Journal of Education and Work, 29*(7), 747-766. doi: 10.1080/13639080.2015.1051520

Bäckman, O., & Nilsson, A. (2016). Long-term consequences of being not in employment, education, or training as a young adult: Stability and change in three Swedish birth cohorts. *European Societies, 18*(2), 136-157. doi: 10.1080/14616696.2016.1153699

Brown, P. (2013). Education, opportunity and the prospects for social mobility. *British Journal of Sociology of Education, 34*(5-6), 678-700. doi: 10.1080/01425692.2013.816036

Brown, P., Green, A., & Lauder, H. (2001). *High skills: Globalization, competitiveness, and skill formation.* Oxford University Press.

Clandinin, D. J. (2013). *Engaging in narrative inquiry.* Left Coast Press.

Dougherty, M. (2019). *The Transition from Post-Secondary Education to Work: Power, Performativity, and Entanglement in Becoming Social Service Workers* [Doctoral dissertation, Simon Fraser University]. http://summit.sfu.ca/item/18950

Dougherty, M. (2021). Reflections: The relational practice of teaching and learning. *Reflections: Narratives of Professional Helping, 27*(1), 49-63.

Dougherty, M. (2022). Reconceptualising the transition from post-secondary education to work. *Journal of Education and Work, 35*(3), 241-255. https://doi-org.proxy.lib.sfu.ca/10.1080/13639080.2022.2048251

Ferguson, S. J., & Wang, S. (2014). *Graduating in Canada: Profile, labour market outcomes and student debt of the class of 2009-2010* (Statistics Canada Publication Catalogue no. 81-595-M — No. 2014101). Canada. Retrieved from: http://www.statcan.gc.ca/pub/81-595-m/81-595-m2014101-eng.pdf

Grubb, W. N. & Lazerson, M. (2004). *The education gospel: The economic power of schooling.* Harvard University Press.

Hull, G. A. (1993). Critical literacy and beyond: Lessons learned from students and workers in a vocational program and on the job. *Anthropology and Education Quarterly, 24*(4), 373-396. https://www-jstor-org.proxy.lib.sfu.ca/stable/3195937

Kincheloe, J. L. (1995). *Toil and trouble: Good work, smart workers, and the integration of academic and vocational education.* Peter Lang Publishing.

Koen, J., Klehe, U-C., & Van Vianen, A. E. (2012). Training career adaptability to facilitate a successful school-to-work transition. *Journal of Vocational Behavior, 81*(3), 395-408. doi: 10.1016/j.jvb.2012.10.003

Lang, M. (2010). Can mentoring assist in the school-to-work transition? *Education + Training, 52*(5), 359-367. doi: 10.1108/00400911011058307

Lehmann, W. (2019). Forms of capital in working-class students' transition from university to employment. *Journal of Education and Work, 32*(4), 347-359. doi: 10.1080/13639080.2019.1617841

Ogbuanya, T. C., & Chukwuedo, S. O. (2017). Career-training mentorship intervention using the Dreyfus model: Implications for career behaviors and practical skills acquisition in vocational electronic technology. *Journal of Vocational Behavior, 103*(B), 88-105. doi: 10.1016/j.jvb.2017.09.002

Pinquart, M., Juang, L., & Silbereisen, R. (2003). Self-efficacy and successful school-to-work transition: A longitudinal study. *Journal of Vocational Behavior, 63*(3), 329-346. doi: 10.1016/S0001-8791(02)00031-3

Renn, R. R., Steinbauer, R., Taylor, R., & Detwiler, D. (2014). School-to-work transition: Mentor career supports and student career planning, job search intentions, and self-defeating job search behaviour. *Journal of Vocational Behavior, 85*(3), 422-432. doi: 10.1016/j.jvb.2014.09.004

Urciuoli, B. (2008). Skills and selves in the new workplace. *American Ethnologist, 35*(2), 211-228. https://www-jstor-org.proxy.lib.sfu.ca/stable/27667485

Valadez, J. R. (2000). Searching for a path out of poverty: Exploring the achievement ideology of a rural community college. *Adult Education Quarterly, 50*(3), 212-230. https://doi-org.proxy.lib.sfu.ca/10.1177/07417130022087017

Vuolo, M., Staff, J., & Mortimer, J. T. (2012). Weathering the Great Recession: Psychological and behavioural trajectories in the transition from school to work. *Developmental Psychology, 48*(6), 1759-1773. doi: 10.1037/a0026047

Yang, N., Yaung, H., Noh, H., Jang, S., & Lee, B. (2017). The change of planned happenstance skills and its association with career-related variables during school-to-work transition. *International Journal for Education and Vocational Guidance, 17*(1), 19-38. doi: 10.1007/s10775-016-9332-z

Chapter 2

The Purpose of Education
and its Relationship to Work

It is widely believed that the primary purpose of education is to prepare people for work. This belief is made visible in marketing campaigns that highlight the employment rates of recent graduates. It can be observed at education fairs for students and their families, where parents evaluate potential schools or programs by asking what jobs their children can get and how much money they will be making. Assumptions about the role of education in preparing students for work are clear when schools place expectations on students to identify their career goals in early secondary school and then tailor their education around this goal. Students calculate the time, energy, and money necessary to obtain certain credentials, weighing out which option has the best return on investment in terms of future employment and income (see Cox, 2009). Depending on their discipline and the institution's focus, educators also see their role, to varying extents, as preparing students for work. It is so ingrained in our understanding that we don't often question that education serves primarily as a pathway to work. However, it wasn't always this way.

The Purpose of Education

As a pathway to employment, education can provide both societal (public) and individual (private) benefits, serving both a private and public good (Labaree, 1997). Different views on the purpose of education have prevailed in the discourse at different times. Examining the changing values of students over a thirty-year period (from 1966 to 1996), Astin (1998) noted a significant shift in the identified priorities of students. Throughout the 1970s and 1980s, students' goals in obtaining an education shifted from "developing a meaningful philosophy of life" to "being very well off financially" (Astin, 1998, p. 124). For students, the purpose of education shifted from a critical examination of life to being a pathway to financial success. Students articulated that "the chief benefit of a college education is to increase one's earning power" and that they were attending college "to be able to make more money" (Astin, 1998, p. 125). As seen in this study, the prevalent view of the purpose of education shifted from education being a public good to education as a private good (Labaree, 1997). Education became a means for social mobility rather than promoting democratic equality and preparing students for citizenship. Educational credentials became an asset or commodity held by an individual, giving them a "competitive advantage ... for desirable social positions" (Labaree, 1997, p. 42). Students' perspectives shifted to see education as a personal asset that would allow them to get a good job, make more money, and be successful.

As education became viewed as a means to employment (i.e., promoting social mobility), it became predominantly viewed as a private good (i.e., an asset held by an individual). According to Grubb and Lazerson (2004), formalized post-secondary education expanded by emphasizing the public benefits of increased education, including enhancing the national economy and promoting equality and opportunity. However, in the mid-1800s, "the synthesis of moral, civic, and intellectual purposes in higher education eroded, eventually giving way to professional goals" (Grubb & Lazerson, 2004, p. 58). By the mid-1900s, education became increasingly focused on professional preparation and served to standardize professional knowledge and expertise (Grubb & Lazerson, 2004). Grubb and Lazerson (2004) explain that as education claimed a monopoly over entry into professions (p. 64), students attended post-secondary for the opportunity it provided for individual gain.

Understanding education as a private good that promotes social mobility occurred within the context of the rise of neo-liberal ideology. During this time, the figureheads of early neoliberalism, like Margaret Thatcher and Ronald Reagan, promoted laissez-faire economics and the primacy of the free market. This means the market is deregulated and operates with minimal government interference (Saunders, 2014; Mc-Laren, 2007). Laissez-faire economics is built on the assumption that the market self-regulates and operates fairly, rewarding people according to their effort (Peters, 2013). Within a neoliberal framework, social structures traditionally regulated by the state—like education—are left to market forces to regulate. All social relations are reduced to market-based terms through processes of marketization and commodification (Ball, 2012a, p. 3). That is, education becomes a commodity that is regulated by the free market. The marketization of social structures, such as education, is accompanied by a focus on profit and capital accumulation (Ball, 2012a; Levin, 2005). Educational institutions compete with one another for students/consumers, operating as businesses that emphasize efficiency and the bottom line (i.e., profit accumulation). This process of marketization and commodification is justified as a necessary and inevitable outcome of a global, capitalist society.

When education is marketized and commodified, educational institutions need to compete for survival. Since the late 20th century, public funding for education has decreased substantially (Levin, 2005), resulting in educational institutions competing for students and other sources of funding (for example, research funding and endowments). In addition to tuition increases, institutions attempt to make up for lost government funding through internationalization, tuition fee differentials, creating and marketing programs and delivery methods popular with student consumers, and privatizing previously funded programs (Levin, 2005). As public funding decreased, post-secondary institutions sought additional funding through entrepreneurial activities, such as corporate sponsorships, endowments, and commercialized research (Rose, 2014). When public institutions accept these forms of private funding, it impacts neutral and objective research and influences to whom the institution is indebted (Kirby, 2007; Rose, 2014). As Rose (2014) argues, corporate sponsorships and educational endowments are tax-deductible. Hence, individuals and corporations build a positive public image by giving to education while avoiding paying taxes that could be used to improve other public services that could significantly impact disadvantaged groups. From this perspective, sponsorships and endowments can restrict academic freedom within an institution and negatively affect other publicly funded social systems.

As institutions must compete in the market, so must the neoliberal student. Consistent with neoliberal ideology, education is an individual opportunity that creates individual rewards; thus, the responsibility to fund higher education shifts to the student. Education becomes financially inaccessible to many students or results in crippling student debt loads (see Giroux, 2014). When education is viewed as a meritocracy, students must compete to differentiate themselves and get ahead of others. Within the myth of meritocracy, more competitive and capable students will have access to elite educational institutions and subsequently obtain employment that is more desirable; there is an assumption that everyone begins at the same starting line in this competition. The fact that students have unequal access to the social, economic, and cultural capital required to be competitive and capable is not examined within neoliberal discourse. An inability to compete is seen as a personal character deficit—for example, the student is lazy or irresponsible—rather than an impact of complex systemic inequalities. Rather than examining the roles that education and employment serve in reproducing social inequality, blame is placed on the individual student (Giroux, 2014). As discussed in Chapter One, much of our understanding of transition derives from an intervention-focused approach that emphasizes student deficit and individual responsibility without adequate critiques of the purpose of education or the realities of work.

Within this environment of competition, a managerial culture (Bergquist & Pawlak, 2007) pervades universities and colleges. The managerial culture involves efficiency, standardization, and performativity (Arvast, 2006; Kirby, 2007). Given the focus on the financial bottom line, efficiency is vitally important; institutions must minimize cost and maximize output (in standardized measures) to remain competitive. Standardization involves ensuring similar products and consistency in markets to allow for standardized outcome measures, comparison, and the maintenance of integrity (Arvast, 2006). In keeping with market principles, provinces are emphasizing quantification, testing, and measurable outcomes; this creates a focus on measures of quality (Levin, 2001; Kirby, 2007) and performativity (Arvast, 2006), where outputs and outcomes are benchmarked, measured, and improved upon (Ball, 2012b). Standardization and performativity can reshape the work of faculty members as they "re-orient pedagogical and scholarly activities towards those which are likely to have a positive impact on measurable performance outcomes and ... (deflect) attention away from aspects of social, emotional or moral development that have no immediate, measurable performative value" (Ball, 2012b, p. 20). The quality measures examined may be economically motivated efficiency measures rather than an actual examination of educational quality. Although education may serve a use-value—such that the content and curriculum is useful in itself—within the managerial culture, institutions emphasize a marketable product (i.e., credential) that students see as valuable for its exchange value.

As education is increasingly marketized, creating a commodity that requires minimal state intervention and can be left to the market to regulate, the role of students changes. Marketization occurs when social and human interests in education are displaced by market principles, like competition and profit, and students become consumers (Kirby, 2007; Levin, 2005) and commodities (Levin, 2005; Urciuoli, 2008; Saunders & Ramirez, 2017). When education is commodified, students become consumers or purchasers of the educational product; programs and delivery methods are marketed towards their preferences rather than learning needs (Ball, 2012b). With this change in role, the emphasis can shift from "teaching a student" to "satisfying a customer". Urciuoli (2008) articulately explains that students are also being increasingly commodified through the educational process and encouraged to become a bundle of employable skills. That is, students are encouraged to see themselves as products to be sold to prospective employers. Commodification promotes skills as discrete units of knowledge that one obtains through education and holds in relation to productive job performance (Urciuoli, 2008). Urciuoli (2008) conducted a discourse analysis of internet sites marketing skill-related services and found that the concept of "skill" has shifted from skilled labour (i.e., apprenticeship, craft mastery) to the internalization of ideals of being a disciplined worker; these ideas correspond to cultural values in the United States, including being self-directed, self-improving, and striving for social mobility. Urciuoli (2008) concludes: "new workers are seen, and are encouraged to see themselves, as bundles of skills anticipating company needs, readily adaptable and subject to assessment", such that identity is reduced to the ability to labour (p. 219). From this perspective, education involves the commodification of students; students internalize the ideals of a 'disciplined worker' and sell themselves as a bundle of employable skills.

Within the neoliberal context of competition, marketization, managerialism, and commodification, social mobility discourse reinforces the assumption that education is a pathway to employment and financial success. From the social mobility perspective, the student is a consumer, and education is a commodity, subject to principles of supply and demand like any other commodity (Labaree, 1997). Rather than serving a use-value (i.e., the curriculum and learning are useful in themselves), education has exchange value; education provides a credential that can be exchanged for desirable employment that promotes status attainment. The social mobility perspective frames education as a meritocracy, where those who demonstrate the most merit will be rewarded. On the face of it, it seems like common sense: those who work hard and achieve good grades will have access to the best employment options. However, social mobility requires inequality. Educational consumers want the best—the school with the best reputation, highest rankings, rockstar professors, and the most comprehensive extra-curricular opportunities—to set themselves apart from others. Social mobility is premised on some having opportunities that others do not; this promotes intense competition and places personal responsibility on students disadvantaged due to systemic factors. Social mobility discourse focuses on the supply-side of employment, promising lucrative employment and "desirable social positions" to the winners of our educational competition (Labaree, 1997, p. 42). But does success in education allow for employment and social mobility? Does the labour market support this promise? The realities of work need to be investigated.

The Realities of Work

Social mobility discourse assumes inequity can be addressed through intergenerational improvements in one's social class, such that one's class origin no longer predicts their destination (Brown, 2013). Brown (2013) articulately deconstructs the concept of social mobility, differentiating between absolute and relative social mobility. Absolute social mobility involves improving one's social standing through a structural expansion in available positions; this occurred in the 1950s and 1960s when there was a substantial expansion of professional and managerial positions (Brown, 2013). On the other hand, relative social mobility depends upon building individual capital and commodifying oneself to be competitive in the crowd. Approaches promoting equity through relative social mobility are often deficit-focused interventions that attempt to increase the employability of disadvantaged groups; this includes equitable access to affordable education (Brown 2013). The promise that education leads to a good job and, thus, a good life incorrectly assumes that demand for high-skilled, educated workers exceeds supply. This is not the case. As stated by Deil-Amen and DeLuca (2010):

> Highly skilled technical labor does not dominate the labor market, and the stable pattern of less than a third of jobs requiring a postsecondary credential is predicted to continue into the foreseeable future. Further, nearly half of the fastest-growing occupations require less than a bachelor's (BA) degree. (p. 27)

Livingstone's (2019) examination of labour market trends reveals similar patterns of educated workers exceeding supply and underemployment in Canada. There are fewer highly skilled positions available, yet increasing numbers of educated people (i.e., people with post-secondary credentials) are seeking those positions. Where positions do require post-secondary credentials, they are regularly filled by employees with more advanced credentials than are required (Livingstone, 2019). Mass education decreases the exchange value of credentials and increases competition for limited available positions. Therefore, rather than promoting relative social mobility, education creates *social congestion* (Brown, 2013, p. 683). Social congestion occurs when the labour market lacks the capacity for an increase in capable, educated workers, and there is more competition for fewer available positions. The result of fewer highly skilled positions is an increase in under-employment in terms of time, skill, and knowledge (Livingstone, 2019). That is, people must resort to working part-time hours when seeking full-time work and/or accept positions that underutilize the knowledge they have obtained through education (Livingstone, 2019).

Not only is relative social mobility unrealistic, it is also unlikely that there will be an increase in available skilled positions (i.e., absolute social mobility). Instead, due to several structural factors, including globalization and increased automation, there is likely to be downward absolute mobility, meaning people will struggle to maintain the social class of the previous generation (Brown, 2013).

There is widening disparity in labour market opportunities as growth is occurring in bottom-tier and top-tier jobs but not in the middle (Ireland, 2015). The implications of this U-shaped pattern are growth in low-skilled, poorly paid jobs, and the number of working poor; racialized employment opportunities with Black, Latino, and immigrant workers concentrated in the bottom tiers; the greater disparity between rich and poor and a diminishing middle class; and fewer opportunity for workers to progress into better positions (Ireland, 2015). Rhetoric pushing students into higher education for employment results in over-credentialling, underemployment, and social congestion (Grubb, 1985; Brown, 2013). There is a surplus of educated student/workers available for a finite number of positions commensurate with their skills. This often leads to students accepting positions for which they are overqualified (in terms of educational background) and being under-employed.

In the hegemonic discourse in higher education, students are promised that achieving a credential will provide the opportunity for 'good' employment that promotes social and economic mobility. Labour market realities do not support this promise of social mobility. The problem is that education is promoted as a ladder of opportunity, where students can empower themselves and rise above their current social strata promoting the opportunity for advancement; critical theorists argue that this is a lie that is perpetuated to keep people in their existing social positions.

The Myth of Meritocracy

Critical scholars[1] argue against the idea that education serves as a pathway to success, troubling fundamental concepts in education like competition and meritocracy. Instead, critical scholars view education as a tool that disciplines students into docile workers to meet the needs of capital. Critical scholars argue that the discourse of social mobility, with its emphasis on personal responsibility, competition, and meritocracy, effectively hides the reproduction of inequality perpetuated by education (e.g., Giroux, 2014). Education promotes stratifying students in keeping with their existing social position.

Proponents of critical pedagogy critique popular discourse that school is a fundamentally democratic institution that is politically neutral and serves to educate the masses by transmitting essential, factual information. They problematize key con-

---

1   Although a diverse group of academics, critical scholars are grouped to demonstrate an alternate perspective on the purpose of schooling focused on relations of power and the effects of discourse. I recognize this generalization and see it as necessary within the confines of this book.

cepts of schooling, including knowledge, curriculum, testing, and classification (McLaren, 2007; Kincheloe, 2004). They further explore the disciplinary nature of schooling (Foucault, 1979) and are committed to developing education to fulfill an emancipatory function (Freire, 1993; McLaren, 2007; Apple, 2004). Critical scholars examine multiple forms of knowledge, question why some knowledge forms are valued over others, and expose the process of knowledge creation as a political process, which reveals power dynamics in terms of what information is selected and what information is silenced (Kincheloe, 2004; Buras & Apple, 2006). Critical scholars argue that education serves to meet the needs of capital by training students efficiently and effectively towards a specific occupation, without problematizing what knowledge is, what learning is necessary, or how the educational process is politicized (Apple, 1999; McLaren, 2007). Within a neoliberal state, education takes on the role of indoctrinating people to take up as "appropriate and appropriated subjects" (Davies & Bansel, 2007, p. 248). School is highly regulated, classified, and disciplined (Foucault, 1979) and 'learning' prioritizes classroom and behaviour management rather than unpacking and critically examining information (McLaren, 2007). Learning becomes a process whereby teachers provide standardized information, which is accepted as 'Truth' and reinforces the dominant culture, and quality is measured through standardized assessment (McLaren, 2007).

Critical theorists speak back against claims that education promotes social mobility and can serve to reduce inequity. Instead, these scholars argue that the discourse of social mobility effectively hides the reproduction of inequity perpetuated by education for social efficiency purposes (e.g., Giroux, 2014). The social efficiency perspective states that school prepares people for work and that assuming certain economic roles is necessary for a healthy economy (Labaree, 1997). Education builds human capital and creates "workers to fill structurally necessary market roles" (Labaree, 1997, p. 42). These market roles may not be desirable jobs but are necessary for social and economic functioning so that the nation can be competitive on a global scale. That is, it is socially beneficial for education to differentially prepare students to fill various roles. A social efficiency perspective recognizes that inequality is necessary for the public good; schooling, thus, socializes students to adapt to the stratified social structure and the demands of the labour market (Labaree, 1997). Within a social efficiency perspective, there is no examination of the labour market nor questioning of the nature of work. The demand side of educational supply (i.e., work) is viewed as fundamentally sound, and the responsibility lies with educational institutions to be responsive to the labour market. Social efficiency requires a highly stratified educational system that reflects the stratification in the labour market. It serves to track students into various occupational positions, reproducing existing social stratification and inequalities.

Working from a critical perspective, Dougherty (2001) discusses conflicting views on the social benefit of education by examining the role of community college in the United States. He explains that while some argue that college was designed to serve the community, providing opportunity through training for mid-level jobs, promising social mobility, and providing a democratizing function through low-cost, open-door access, others see college as reproducing class inequities in a capitalist society (Dougherty, 2001). From this perspective, workers are trained at public expense for private profit and are diverted away from four-year institutions, ensuring that working-class children maintain their oppressed social position (Brint & Karabel, 1991). Colleges then help preserve the selectivity of four-year institutions, promote the "cooling out" of students (Clark, 1980), and protect the exchange value of credentials in training employees for the workforce (Dougherty, 2001). Rather than promote democratic equality, education serves to protect the privileged in a stratified and unequal society by tracking students into less desirable educational opportunities (e.g., college, vocational and training programs, etc.), which align to socially necessary employment in keeping with social efficiency.

Levin's (2001) research on community colleges in the United States and Canada also highlights how social efficiency goals are framed within discourses of democratic equality. While the community college provides increased access to post-secondary education (through less stringent admission requirements and lowered tuition costs), promoting democratic equality, it also tracks students into specific employment opportunities in keeping with social efficiency. Levin (2001) analyzed federal and state/provincial policy in the United States (i.e., Hawaii, California, and Washington) and Canada (i.e., British Columbia and Alberta) to examine how globalization and neoliberal government policies impacted community colleges. He found that policy has shifted the mission of community college towards economic goals; he sees the focus shifting from democratic equality goals of access, personal and social development, and general education to social efficiency goals of workplace training, producing a globally competitive workforce, and providing specific skill acquisition. Within federal and state/provincial policies, governments emphasize the community college as a "globally competitive business", with reduced public sector funding and subject to the elements of globalization (Levin, 2001). Levin (2001) found that Canadian institutions were more closely aligned with government ideology, noting that these institutions operated as an extension of the state. In sum, "serving the community—a foundational principle of community colleges in both countries—can be viewed as a euphemism for supporting the interests of a neo-liberal state with its devotion to private sector business and industry" (Levin, 2001, p. 258).

How does this Influence our Understanding of School to Work Transition?

Neoliberal ideology shapes the world in which we all live. We accept as natural that we must compete with one another for our own success. Although largely unstated, we assume that education, specifically post-secondary education, is the pathway to individual and societal success. And, as stated, we see in examples all around us how that assumption is enacted by students and within educational institutions. There is also an assumption in the social mobility discourse that desirable employment is available to those who work hard and achieve an appropriate credential. However, mass education creates social congestion and underemployment rather than promoting social mobility. The false portrayal of school as a meritocracy serves to reproduce inequalities by placing individual blame on students for un/underemployment without problematizing structural constraints that limit student options, including labour market realities (Giroux, 2014; Ireland, 2015; Valadez, 2000). The myth of social mobility benefits the ruling class through the discipline and indoctrination of workers that will fill the needs of the labour market, in line with social efficiency perspectives.

Critically exploring the purpose of education and labour market realities that limit employment opens different perspectives on transition. How do students experience their transition from post-secondary education to work? How do those working from an ethics of care experience the neoliberal institutions of school and work? What does 'success' look like to students who transition into care-oriented work, like social service work? To open the concept of transition further, I examined the transition experiences of social service workers. Working in social services involves putting the needs of people who live very precarious lives and have been discarded by society at the forefront. I wondered how students may transition into this role, focusing on others, given that the institutions of post-secondary education and work emphasize individualism and competition. I was curious how students—like my students—transition from post-secondary education to working in social services.

In my observation, students approach their education very instrumentally; they express pressure for timely completion, the need to graduate, the importance of achieving a credential, and the stress of making the 'right' choices with respect to courses, specializations, practicum experiences, volunteering, and work experience. Given their instrumental approach to education, I was especially interested in how students experienced the transition from post-secondary education to social service work. How were their values, beliefs, education, experiences, and sense of self challenged by the actualities of work in a helping profession? What tensions did they bump up against in navigating educational and employment expectations and responsibilities? How did they see themselves as a 'student' and a 'worker', and how were those identities enacted across different contexts? How could plugging into their transition experience provide new ways of thinking about relating, helping, teaching, and education? As discussed in detail in Chapter 3, exploring the tensions social service workers experience as they transition into their professional roles can offer something new to our understanding of school to work transition.

References

Apple, M. W. (1999). Freire, neo-liberalism and education. *Discourse, 20*(1), 5-20. doi: 10.1080/0159630990200101

Apple, M. (2004). *Ideology and curriculum* (3rd ed.). Routledge.

Arvast, A. (2006). From community to commodity college: Globalization, neoliberalism and the new

Ontario college curricula. *Canadian Journal of Educational Administration and Policy, 50.* Retrieved from: http://www.umanitoba.ca/publications/cjeap/pdf_files/arvast.pdf

Astin, A. W. (1998). The changing American college student: Thirty-year trends, 1966-1996. *The Review of Higher Education, 21*(2), 115-134.

Ball, S. J. (2012a). *Global education Inc.: New policy networks and the neo-liberal imaginary.* Routledge.

Ball, S. J. (2012b). Performativity, commodification and commitment: An I-spy guide to the neoliberal university. *British Journal of Educational Studies, 60*(1), 17-28. doi: 10.1080/00071005.2011.650940

Bergquist, W., & Pawluk, K. (2007). *Engaging the six cultures of the academy: Revised and expanded version of the four cultures of the academy.* Jossey-Bass.

Brint, S., & Karabel, J. (1989). *Diverted dream: Community college and the promise of educational opportunity in America, 1900-1985.* Oxford University Press.

Brown, P. (2013). Education, opportunity and the prospects for social mobility. *British Journal of Sociology of Education, 34*(5-6), 678-700. doi: 10.1080/01425692.2013.816036

Buras, K. L., & Apple, M. W. (2006). Introduction. In M. W. Apple and K. L Buras (Eds.), *The subaltern speak: Curriculum, power, and educational struggles* (pp. 1-39). Routledge.

Clark, B. (1980). The "cooling out" function revisited. *New Directions for Community Colleges, 32,* 15-31.

Cox, R. D. (2009). "I would have rather paid for a class I wanted to take": Utilitarian approaches at a community college. *The Review of Higher Education, 32*(3), 353-382. doi: 10.1353/rhe.0.0065

Davies, B., & Bansel, P. (2007). Neoliberalism and education. *International Journal of Qualitative Studies in Education, 20*(3), 247-259. doi: 10.1080/09518390701281751

Deil-Amen, R., & DeLuca, S. (2010). The underserved third: How our educational structures populate an educational underclass. *Journal of Education for Students Placed at Risk, 15,* 27-50. doi: 10.1080/10824661003634948

Dougherty, K. (2001). *The contradictory college: The conflicting origins, impacts, and futures of the community college.* State University of New York Press.

Foucault, M. (1979). *Discipline and punish: The birth of the prison.* (A. Sheridan, Trans.). Vintage.

Freire, P. (1993). *Pedagogy of the oppressed* (20th Anniversary Edition). Penguin Books.

Giroux, H. (2014). *Neoliberalism's war on higher education.* Haymarket Books.

Grubb, W. N. (1985). The convergence of educational systems and the role of vocationalism. *Comparative Education Review, 29*(4), 526-548. https://www-jstor-org.proxy.lib.sfu.ca/stable/1188199

Grubb, W. N. & Lazerson, M. (2004). *The education gospel: The economic power of schooling.* Harvard University Press.

Ireland, S. M. (2015). Fostering success or stratification? A macroapproach to understanding "success" in the community college content. *Community College Journal of Research and Practice, 39*(2), 150-162. doi: 10.1080/10668926.2013.775087

Kincheloe, J. L. (2004). The knowledges of teacher education: Developing a critical complex epistemology. *Teacher Education Quarterly,* Wint, 49-66.

Kirby, D. (2007). Reviewing Canadian post-secondary education: Post-secondary education policy in post-industrial Canada. *Canadian Journal of Educational Administration and Policy, 65.* Retrieved from: http://www.umanitoba.ca/publications/cjeap/pdf_files/kirby.pdfx

Labaree, D. F. (1997). Public goods, private goods: The American struggle over educational goals. *American Educational Research Journal, 34*(1), 39-81. doi: 10.2307/1163342

Levin, J. S. (2001). Public policy, community colleges, and the path to globalization. *Higher Education, 42*(2), 237-262.

Levin, J. S. (2005). The business culture of the community college: Students as consumers; students as commodities. *New Directions for Higher Education, 129,* 11-26. doi: 10.1002/he.169

Livingstone, D. W. (2019). Underemployment of highly qualified labor in advanced capitalism: Trends and prospects. *Journal of Education and Work, 32*(4), 305-319. doi: 10.1080/13639080.2019.1646415

McLaren, P. (2007). *Life in schools: An introduction to critical pedagogy in the foundations of education* (5th Ed.). Pearson Education, Inc.

Peters, M. A. (2013). Managerialism and the neoliberal university: Prospects for new forms of 'open management' in higher education. *Contemporary Readings in Law and Social Justice, 5*(1), 11-26.

Rose, M. (2014). *Why school? Reclaiming education for all of us.* The New Press.

Saunders, D. B. (2014). Exploring a customer orientation: Free-market logic and college students. *The Review of Higher Education, 37*(2), 197-219. doi: 10.1353/rhe.2014.0013

Saunders, D. B., & Ramirez, G. B. (2017). Resisting the neoliberalization of higher education: A challenge to commonsensical understandings of commodities and consumption. *Cultural Studies <-->* *Critical Methodologies, 17*(3), 189-196. doi: 10.1177/1532708616669529

Urciuoli, B. (2008). Skills and selves in the new workplace. *American Ethnologist, 35*(2), 211-228. https://www-jstor-org.proxy.lib.sfu.ca/stable/27667485

Valadez, J. R. (2000). Searching for a path out of poverty: Exploring the achievement ideology of a rural community college. *Adult Education Quarterly, 50*(3), 212-230. https://doi-org.proxy.lib.sfu.ca/10.1177/07417130022087017

Part 2

Transitioning to Social Service Work

Chapter 3

Who are Social Service Workers?

My own experience in social services and my role as an educator with students on a trajectory to work in this field raised questions about the transition experience of students in care-oriented fields. I wondered how the tensions between relational work
and financial indicators of success influenced these students in
school and work. How do students who are learning to work
from an ethics of care experience the transition from post-
secondary to work? To examine this, I differentiated social
service work from social work and other professionalized
fields; being a liminal group plays an important role in social
service workers' school and work experiences. This chapter
explains how I've defined *social service workers* and how
they differ from other professions. I explore why their experiences might open up new understandings of school to work
transitions. This provides a foundation for conceptualizing the
school to work transition differently and offers new potentialities for social service work and education.

First, I need to delineate what a social service worker is
and how they differ from other helping professionals. For the
purposes of this book, social service workers are employed as
front-line workers in community-based not-for-profit agencies. What the social service worker does varies, depending

on their role, the agency they work within, and the people they serve. Generally, social service work involves building caring connections; engaging in informal counselling; providing outreach, information, and referrals; building strengths, competencies, and life skills; and addressing the identified needs of those served. This front-line work may involve working at a drop-in centre for homeless youth, providing warm meals, a shower, clean clothes, a listening ear, and connecting youth to other resources and services. It could also involve working with adults with significant mental health concerns in their own homes to build life skills and independence. It may mean working at a homeless shelter for adults with multiple vulnerabilities—mental health, addiction, and physical health needs—to provide temporary safety and connection to other resources. Social service work is complex in that it involves engaging with all developmental stages and a variety of vulnerabilities in the life space of those served; the role is varied, and social service workers need to adapt and innovate when faced with new situations and challenges.

In this research, I make a distinction between the helping professions from various disciplines, engaging in relational work, and social service workers. Helping professions include those working in health care (e.g., nursing) and social work; these are professionalized fields (i.e., standardized educational qualifications, qualifying exams, registration, etc.) and often result in employment with provincial authorities (i.e., government positions in health care or child welfare). I've chosen to examine workers employed in not-for-profit community-based agencies and exclude those working in government positions. Unlike social work, social service work is not a regulated, professionalized discipline; social service workers come from various academic trajectories and life experiences. There are no standardized educational qualifications for front-line social service work; qualifications are set by each agency based on their mandate, philosophy, the role and responsibilities of the position, and, to a large extent, funding.

Distinct from other helping professions (like social work), there is a lack of standardization in qualifications for social service workers; their academic qualifications range from certificates to baccalaureate degrees. The lack of standardization in front-line social service work creates two distinct and related concerns: the creation of an educational underclass and a transition into more precarious work. Workers in social services are a liminal group. Employment in this field is not well paid or well respected. Government funding for services is tenuous, meaning employment can be unstable. Workers are responsible for working with people who have been expunged by society (e.g., individuals with addiction, mental health concerns, histories of violence, developmental delays, homelessness, and other challenges). By Deil-Amen and DeLuca's (2010) categorization, students engaging in education to obtain employment in social services constitute an "educational underclass"; these are primarily non-traditional students who engage in vocationalized education in colleges or non-elite universities to enter a field marked by tenuous employment. Many of these non-traditional students, in my experience, are first-generation students and those who may not have had positive educational experiences, students who may be receiving funding for retraining (e.g., as a job placement program), and/or students who may have previously received services in the social service system. As there are no standardized educational qualifications for front-line social service work (in contrast to a more professionalized field like social work), these students may be involved in certificate, diploma, or degree programs. While those students who receive a degree (e.g., Bachelor of Social Work, Bachelor of Arts in Child and Youth Care, etc.) have additional opportunities for work in government positions—the students transitioning into community-based non-governmental employment face more precarious employment.

Butler (2009) relates precarity to determining who is recognized as a worthwhile subject; this concept can be applied to the marginalized populations served by social service workers and the social service workers themselves. According to Butler (2009), those who live outside the idealized norm may be marked by precarity, including increased risk of poverty, injury, disease, violence, and death. That is, those living outside of what is deemed acceptable are not recognizable and, subsequently, not worthy subjects. People who receive social services and who are living outside of what is deemed acceptable face poverty, injury, violence, and an increased risk of death. Their lives are precarious; "precarious life characterizes such lives who do not qualify as recognizable, readable, or grievable" (Butler, 2009, p. xii and xiii). Social service workers who work with people with precarious lives also live outside the idealized norm. In their case, social service workers do not ascribe to the idealized norm of success. That is, rather than accept the norm of success being related to financial wealth, social service workers practice from an ethics of care and, consequently, may experience precarity. Like those they serve, social service workers too may face tenuous employment (e.g., contracts, part-time work, lack of benefits) and living environments, transience, and a lack of recognition of the legitimacy of their work. Social service workers exist within a complex arrangement that can regulate them to precarity; this arrangement involves their own history and experiences that they bring to their work, their academic trajectories, the nature of front-line work, the complex needs of those they serve, and the neoliberal institutions they exist within. For these reasons, I was interested in exploring the transition from post-secondary education to working in the field with marginalized people.

In their precarious and often unrecognized work, social service workers face challenges operating from an ethics of care within a competitive and individualistic environment. An ethics of care is rooted in feminist traditions, examining the role of biological sex in moral development and caregiving behaviours (see Gilligan, 1982) and reconceptualizing notions of the public and private spheres (Held, 2006). Social service work is relational; relation, not the individual, is the basis of our existence. Being ethical involves caring (Noddings, 2013); caring emphasizes the importance of relationships and our connections to one another. An ethics of care emphasizes caring encounters, interactions where we are open to sharing, understanding, and reflecting upon the experience of the other and putting our energy toward their needs (Noddings, 2013).

Caring encounters involve connection and reciprocity; although each encounter may involve one caring-for and one cared-for, the one caring-for derives recognition from the cared-for (Noddings, 2013). The one caring-for doesn't enter the encounter for their own benefit yet still derives something from the encounter. Both the cared-for and the one caring leave the encounter different than they were before. Furthermore, the roles of caring and being cared for are fluid and relational; in some encounters, we may be caring for others, while in others, we may be cared for (Noddings, 2013).

Caring in a relationship is the foundation of social service work. To varying extents, social service workers care for marginalized and increasingly complex people in environments that often lack adequate resources; because of reduced services and resources, these workers may be overworked and burdened with high caseloads. Given the people they care for, social service workers are at high risk of developing vicarious trauma or toxic stress (Cohen & Collens, 2013), leading to burnout. In addition to these relational factors, these workers need to navigate working from an ethics of care within a managerial environment. That is, while social service workers need to centre themselves, in relational caring with those they serve, they also must ground their work in an environment that operates under a business model that emphasizes demonstrated efficacy and efficiency.

As the foundational aspect of social service work, caring appears antithetical to neoliberal understandings of individual responsibility, competition, and success. As seen the dominant narrative of competition is incongruent with the emphasis on caring in social service work. So, how do social service workers experience this tension? How do social service workers, working from an ethics of care, navigate the neoliberal education and work institutions, and what do they bump up against in this transition? How can plugging into their narratives open new ways of thinking about the school to work transition?

Exploring the Stories of Social Service Workers

To explore these questions, I engaged in a series of interviews with five social service workers who identified themselves as new to the field of social service work. While, at first look, it may seem simple to introduce the five social service workers and define what it means to be a 'new' social service worker, these are complex processes that influence what we can know. It is important to know who the social service workers (i.e., participants) are but also important to recognize that they are complex, dynamic, and developing and can't be viewed as fixed or knowable. Similarly, being 'new' is not easily quantifiable. I initially looked for participants working in social services for less than one year (which is consistent with existing literature on newly qualified social workers), but I found that defining a participant as 'new' was much more complex than initially conceived. Participants had unique trajectories involving school and work that were not linear or chronological. As social service work is diverse, so too are the experiences of those who work in the field, their role and responsibilities, and the degree of connection they have to the work. The experience of being 'new' is individual and entangled with the participant's unique trajectory involving school and work. The dynamism of the participants and the complexity of being 'new' to social service work highlight the problematics of transition as a linear process with distinct stages (see Ashton & Ashton, 2016; Nairn et al., 2012).

I approached my encounters with the participants as processual, recognizing that we (as participants and researcher) are continually constituted by the discourses and material arrangements of which we are a part. We are works in progress, and the stories shared are also dynamic, developing, and always incomplete. Therefore, I am not describing these individuals to construct them as fixed, stable, coherent, and knowable (Jackson & Mazzei, 2012); instead, I provide some sense of who the participants are, both as unique individuals and members of social groups according to age, gender, ethnicity, academic qualifications, and work experience. These descriptors are based on my observations and the stories shared and are inherently problematic. The research, participants, and researcher are situated in discourse and theory and thus are under constant construction (Bridges-Rhoads & Van Cleave, 2014). I discuss how identities are enacted and performed in more detail in Chapter 5.

Below, I introduce the participants (using pseudonyms) and explain how I approached our encounters and their stories[1]. Here are descriptions of the five participants at the time of the interviews:

Elizabeth is a White woman who graduated from a private, Christian liberal arts university with a Bachelor of Arts in Psychology with a certificate in Human Services. She noted that the program was a combination of psychology and sociology

---

1 I discuss more methodological detail in Appendix A, including an explanation of critical narrative inquiry and my recruitment, interviewing, and analysis processes.

with some similarities to social work and that her degree had applied learning components (i.e., practicum). In her early 20s, she worked as a mental health worker promoting independence for adults living with mental health diagnoses. Elizabeth said she always knew she wanted to work with people and help those facing challenges by recognizing and honouring their humanity. She recognized that being supportive to others, empathic and non-judgmental were important values in her family and that she regularly saw her mother and grandparents enact these values.

Carolyn is a Korean-Canadian woman working at a crisis shelter for youth. She completed her Bachelor of Social Work degree at a large public research institution and spent some time doing church ministry work before moving into social service work in her early 20s. Carolyn also engaged in an international internship before obtaining her current position. Carolyn noted that her education allowed her to reflect on bias and critically examine race, culture, gender, and oppression; she found this social justice perspective congruent to who she is and wanted to work with children and youth to put her values into practice.

Hannah is a White woman who was working as a consultant for inclusivity in community settings. As she explained, she educates child care professionals, empowering them to do their work more inclusively; this includes maximizing ways for children to fully participate, be respected, and preserve their dignity in various settings. Hannah completed her Bachelor of Arts in Child and Youth Care at a large public research institution before doing an international internship. Hannah resided with Carolyn during their internship; the two are best friends, and Hannah agreed to participate in this project at Carolyn's cajoling. Hannah was 24 years old at the time of our interviews.

Alison is a White woman who has a Bachelor of Arts degree in Social Anthropology but returned to school full-time to obtain a Bachelor of Social Work degree from a large, public research institution. Alison was 30 years old, studying full-time and working part-time at a resource centre for street-entrenched youth, struggling with substance use, and/or having mental health concerns. She sought more practical experience and wanted to learn about good relational practices that could help promote systemic change. Alison is committed to continuing to learn, gaining more experience, and improving her practice. She stated that her family is perpetually confused as to why she would return to school to work in a field where she will earn less income than she would with her initial degree.

Matthew is a White male. He was 40 years old at the time of our interviews and working at a group home for adults with developmental disabilities as well as relief work at shelters for homeless adults. Matthew was initially interested in psychiatric nursing but obtained his diploma in Community Social Service Work with a Co-Occurring Disorders Advanced Certificate. He says his educational experience really changed who he is in a positive way and that he was looking at whether he should continue with his education and seek more responsibility within the agencies he works for.

I approached my encounters with Elizabeth, Carolyn, Hannah, Alison, and Matthew, recognizing that the identity of the narrator and their story is under ongoing development (Chase, 2005). My objective for using a narrative inquiry approach was to allow participants to determine what is meaningful and relevant as they engaged in telling, re-living, and re-telling their narrative (Connolly & Clandinin, 1990) in a way that would promote critical awareness of their position and experiences. This approach is consistent with critical paradigms that seek to provide space for multiple subjectivities and voices (Kincheloe, 2008). It also recognizes that embedded within our own individual and social narratives, the participants and

I co-construct meaning through a process of dialogue. The narrator and the narrative are dynamic and continually developing, producing one another; through the process of reliving their narrative, the narrator learns about who they are (Clandinin, 2013; Hull & Zacher, 2007).

As researcher, I recognized that each participant's process of meaning-making is unique and dynamic, and contextualized within a complex life (Clandinin, 2013). In exploring the participants' stories, I examined the social, cultural, political, historical, and institutional narratives in which they occur and how these macro-level narratives shape and influence individual experiences (Clandinin, 2013). I analyzed participant narratives understanding the power of the narrative; a narrative can be disruptive in its ability to demonstrate the social, cultural, historical, and political constraints that limit an individual's range of options for the construction of self and reality (Chase, 2005). A narrative can also promote social justice by highlighting the creativity and complexity of how people construct themselves within their world, despite these powerful constraints, pointing to new possibilities for living in the world.

In keeping with my ethical responsibility, I hoped to determine how the participant narratives could disrupt hegemonic, oppressive processes and promote social justice and democracy; I sought to examine, as Clandinin (2013) describes, how these narratives "bump up" against existing narratives, creating tension and revealing new understandings.

How Might These Stories Open New Understandings of School to Work Transition?

As explored above, social service workers often come from an educational underclass and practice an ethics of care in precarious, complex, and challenging relational work. Constituted in dominant neoliberal discourse, social service workers navigate the institutions of school and work, and the tensions in their experiences help highlight the incongruence of traditional understandings of transition. Examining social service work and the challenges of transitioning into social service work helps complexify the dominant view of the transition from post-secondary education to work as a linear, distinct event that can be assessed through primarily financial indicators.

Complexifying our understanding of transition as critical scholars/educators and practitioners allows us to move beyond deficit-focused interventions. It offers a more comprehensive understanding of how factors beyond the individual student constitute and constrain the transition experience. As discussed throughout Part 2, the social service workers' narratives of navigating the neoliberal institutions of school and work highlight power relations, idealized expectations, and the experience of transition as an ongoing process. Their narratives illustrate the importance of resistance, criticality, and exploring alternate discourses of what it means to 'successfully transition' into a professional role. Examining the social service workers' experiences through the concepts of power, performativity, and becoming allows taken-for-granted assumptions of transition to be re-imagined in ways that can influence how we are with one another in classrooms, in the field, and beyond.

References

Ashton, H. S., & Ashton, D. N. (2019). "Bring on the dancers": Reconceptualising the transition from school to work. *Journal of Education and Work, 29*(7), 747-766. doi: 10.1080/13639080.2015.1051520

Butler, J. (2009). Performativity, precarity, and sexual politics. *AIBR - Revista de Antropología Iberoamericana, 4*(3), 321-336. doi: 10.11156/aibr.040303e

Chase, S. E. (2005). Narrative inquiry: Multiple lenses, approaches, voices. In N. K. Denzin and Y. S. Lincoln (Eds.), *The Sage handbook of qualitative research* (3rd ed.) (pp. 651-679). SAGE Publications.

Clandinin, D. J. (2013). *Engaging in narrative inquiry.* Left Coast Press.

Cohen, K., & Collens, P. (2013). The impact of trauma work on trauma workers: A metasynthesis on vicarious trauma and vicarious posttraumatic growth. *Psychological Trauma: Theory, Research, Practice, and Policy, 5*(6), 570-580. doi: 10.1037/a0030388

Connolly, F. M., & Clandinin, D. J. (1990). Stories of experience and narrative inquiry. *Educational Researcher, 19*(5), 2-14.

Deil-Amen, R., & DeLuca, S. (2010). The underserved third: How our educational structures populate an educational underclass. *Journal of Education for Students Placed at Risk, 15*, 27-50. doi: 10.1080/10824661003634948

Gilligan, C. (1982). *In a different voice: Psychological theory and women's development.* Harvard University Press.

Held, V. (2006). *The ethics of care: Personal, political, and global.* Oxford University Press.

Hull, G., & Zacher, J. (2007). Enacting identities: An ethnography of a job training program. *International Journal of Theory and Research, 7*(1), 71-102. doi: 10.1080/15283480701319708

Jackson, A. Y., & Mazzei, L. A. (2012). *Thinking with theory in qualitative research: Viewing data across multiple perspectives.* Routledge.

Kincheloe, J. L. (2008). *Critical pedagogy* (2nd ed). Peter Lang Publishing.

Nairn, K., Higgins, J., & Sligo, J. (2012). *Children of Rogernomics: A neoliberal generation leaves school.* Otago University Press.

Noddings, N. (2013). *Caring: A relational approach to ethics and moral education.* University of California Press.

Chapter 4

"I Should be Further Ahead"—Power Relations in Transition

The participant narratives provide insight into the transition from school to working in social services. The most prevalent theme in the narratives is the pressure that the participants' felt to succeed, to get somewhere fast. They discuss the omnipresent pressure to be further ahead and discuss comparing themselves to others, and internalizing responsibility when they assess themselves as coming up short. The concept of *power* allows for a nuanced examination of how the neoliberal pressures of competition and success constrain and constitute social service workers in transition and provides potentialities for resistance. Here, I examine the participants' experiences of pressure to succeed and how they question and critique these pressures and draw from alternative discourses to reframe their experiences.

The discourse of social mobility weaves through participants' narratives of how education is viewed as a 'pathway to success'; their discussions affirm the view that receiving a credential provides access to meaningful and profitable employment and ultimately, a good life. Most participants discussed the pressures, both internal and external, to 'achieve'; to possess certain material goods and to be envied in their personal and professional capacities–to 'succeed'. Matthew discussed how he had internalized the pressure to succeed from family and friends, comparing himself to his previous classmates who have achieved additional credentials and are working in more advanced positions. He focused on the financial aspects of work—desiring an increase in hourly wage; ensuring he works adequate shifts to maintain a certain income; working close to home to limit the time, energy, and financial costs of commuting–and whether engaging in additional education is "worth it", financially. In discussing the pressure from others to return to school, he stated:

> The choices I make have to be my own. They have to be well thought out—especially financially. I feel a lot of pressure to make the right choices financially, especially considering the amount of money people are paid in this industry right now.

Carolyn also discussed the pressure to 'succeed' as a competition to be more successful than others. She articulated the need to "be somewhere fast" and asked, "but where?" She explained that although she was unsure where she was supposed to be, she felt like she was not measuring up, not doing enough:

> I still feel elements of competition. Being back in Canada after my internship, I look around at my peers. I should be further ahead. Where is my house? We are very competitive in Western countries. You are always feeling like you are not doing enough, that I am not enough. We all feel that pressure to be somewhere fast or be successful in something but where? For who? I worry about the pressure when your friends are getting married, their careers, or people in accounting who are making good money; you're like, I better step my game up.

Carolyn felt pressure when she compared herself to her friends who have met social milestones, including getting married and having lucrative careers. She felt she needs to "step her game up", suggesting she does not feel she is 'enough'. Her lack of career stability and wealth is presented as a personal failure or character defect. In comparing herself to her friends, Carolyn addresses material elements of success. In Carolyn's discussion, she noted competition is a cultural value in Western countries; she stated that she became increasingly aware of competition within Canadian culture after returning from an internship in Africa. Her discussion highlights the relationship between pressure to succeed (as a physical and affective force) and the materiality of wealth. Western cultural values of competition and consumerism are consistent with the neoliberal ideology that emphasizes personal responsibility, individualism, and meritocracy.

Alison noted similar experiences of pressure to compete based on comparisons with family members:

> I am 30, and I have never made more than $16,000 per year. I have almost $60,000 in student loan debt. I have never been able to pay off any of it. I come from a family deeply entrenched in poverty—both of my parents have been on permanent disability for over 10 years. My dad worked in street ministries and got donations from the church; he didn't have a salary for most of my life. I live in a basement suite that is definitely illegal. That place will be renovicted any day. They get closed down if they are not suitable for people to live in; they are open to inspections, and this neighbourhood has been under examination. It is constantly precarious. So, I compare that to my cousins who went through college into $50,000–$70,000 per year jobs, minimum. My 27-year-old cousin is on his fourth mortgage and has been married for eight years. He bought a house at the age of 19. That is the norm in my family. For me, deciding to go back to school for a career that pays less than the degree I had to begin with at the age of 28—everyone thought I was nuts. I feel like there are all of these social expectations of where you ought to be when you're 30. You should have at

least started an RRSP!

Alison noted that her immediate family was deeply entrenched in poverty and that she now resides in a precarious living situation due to her limited income and substantial student loan debt. She later compared herself to her cousin, who first bought a house at the age of 19, explaining that this is the norm within her extended family. Alison's family is both entrenched in poverty and is made up of members who move from college into high-paying jobs, marriages, and mortgages; this demonstrates the complexity of lives and incomes. She noted that social expectations are associated with age; she is 30 years old, not married, and her comment about starting a Registered Retirement Savings Plan (RRSP) and having a mortgage is steeped in irony. She recognized that, at her age, the expectation (from somewhere beyond herself, swirling in neoliberal discourse) is that she should be planning for the future and retirement; Alison's reality is much more tenuous and focused on immediate needs. Alison is focused on maintaining her residence and meeting her daily needs on a part-time income while taking a full course load and preparing for practicum. Alison did not have financial assistance from her immediate family, which is integral for members of her generation to live outside of precarity. She compared herself to her cousin, who is an anomaly in his financial stability. Although Alison's challenges in living independently seem to be common with members of her generation, she internalizes her precarious work and housing as flowing from her own choices and from not being 'enough'.

Similar to Carolyn, Matthew shared his desire to get somewhere and "to get there fast", although he was also unclear on the destination. Like Alison, Matthew has internalized his lack of perceived success as flowing from his own actions. Below, Matthew described where he is, in relation to his current work and how he is responsible for changing his current situation:

Overall, I'm happy. Sometimes I think I should push more to make more money. I have a pretty good understanding that you don't make more money just because you want to make more money; you have to be willing to take on more responsibility. You better be worth the money you are making. I have impatience to get where I want to go—and I don't even know where that is. But I want to get there fast. Wherever that is. I've pushed myself to work 16 hours per day, going from the shelter to the group home, and sleeping four hours per night. But it isn't sustainable. It would be nice to make another $5 per hour, make a bit more money, work close to home. The positions that are available where you make more money seem a bit beyond my level of experience—I don't know if I just need to suit up and show up.

Matthew, like Carolyn, described the pressure to get some-where quickly while recognizing uncertainty about where he was trying to go. Matthew discussed his feeling of respon-sibility for getting where he wants to go (i.e., taking on more responsibility, making more money, working closer to home, etc.); in this vein, he views his lack of perceived success in achieving a certain position or wage as an individual failure (see Nairn et al., 2012, for similar findings). In Matthew's ex-ample, it is unclear whether more senior positions were avail-able or if there were positions within his field where it would be possible to make an additional $5 per hour. Matthew puts this responsibility upon himself, in keeping with neoliberal values of meritocracy and competition, without examining the structural constraints that may limit his ability to achieve these goals.

Elizabeth discussed the disparity between needing to get somewhere and then, once arriving, wondering if it was worth it. She explained that the pressure to get somewhere seems to continue, despite successfully achieving significant goals;

the goal line keeps moving. Elizabeth discussed the desire to transition from a student to being "a functional adult". She described how she was ready to "not be a student"; she wanted to let go of that identity and be more of an adult. For her, being an adult was not necessarily marked by financial indicators of success in keeping with social mobility discourse and neoliberal ideology; rather, this involved "having a balanced life of going to work, having friends, doing things, living not with family—all of those aspects". She further elucidated that when she was in school, she found being a student all-consuming. To her, being an adult meant being able to spend time with friends, doing things you enjoy, and living independently. However, upon graduation, she questioned whether she had made the right decision to attend post-secondary:

> Really graduation happened and I was like, oh man. I had worked so long and now it is behind you—what do I do now? Did I make a huge mistake and wrack up a bunch of student loans for nothing?

Elizabeth shared that in her current role in social service work: "similar questions come up now. I sometimes look at the job I'm in and ask, could I do this for a while?" Elizabeth's questions highlight that the pressure to get somewhere (e.g., graduating from post-secondary, obtaining a job that aligns with your educational trajectory) does not subside when one actually gets to where they intended; instead, the value of the achievement is questioned, there is disappointment, and a new goal is set.

Matthew, Alison, and Carolyn discussed this pressure to succeed as an external and undifferentiated force; in their experience, "we all" feel "all of these social expectations". When speaking of the successes of friends and family members, they ascribe the pressure they feel to compete with them as social and cultural, noting that "everyone" thinks they should be in a certain and better social and financial place than they are.

Yet I note that although the pressure is described as external, Matthew, Alison, and Carolyn still compare themselves to friends and family members, using specific material measures of 'success'. They have internalized these expectations. Based on their explanations, success involves houses instead of basement suites, well-paying careers instead of jobs, and mortgages instead of student loans. It is interesting that while both student loans and mortgages are forms of debt, mortgages are seen (in these examples) as acceptable and as a sign of success, while student loans are seen as negative and potentially irresponsible. Education, in terms of both its use value and exchange value in the labour market, is seen as a much more valuable "asset" than a material possession that can depreciate in value, but this is not how Carolyn and Alison talked about these forms of debt.

However, these participants also recognized that perhaps the relationship between education and employment was not as clear as they had originally thought. In describing his internal conflict in deciding whether to return to post-secondary for his degree, Matthew examined the relationship between credentials and positions within his workplace:

> I have met a lot of people with [agency name] who have diplomas or sometimes no formal education, and they are in middle management because of their experience and their willingness to do a good job. Then there are brand new casuals with degrees or master's degrees or people who are counsellors who work at the shelter as a second job—there doesn't seem to be any rhyme or reason in terms of who is where in terms of their education and where they sit in the agency. There is no rule to that—so you can't tell me that magically, things will work out for me just because I decide to go back to school for three more years.

Matthew's discussion demonstrates that although some of

the participants seem to be internalizing neoliberal pressures to succeed, they are also questioning, at times, some of these expectations. I saw the participants questioning the pressures they feel and the expectations that are placed upon them (by themselves and by others) as acts of resistance. To help explore this idea, I put Foucault's concept of power to work to help understand how participants deconstruct these expectations and practices, question their origin, and resist neoliberal conceptualizations of success as natural and inevitable and flowing from individual choice and competition. I review Foucault's concept of power to then analyze the participants' narratives of resistance to neoliberal discourses and definitions of 'success'.

Foucault's Conceptualization of Power

For Foucault, power is not a characteristic held by an individual. Instead, power is a productive force that is relational and works both on and through people. Foucault (1979) states: "In fact, power produces; it produces reality; it produces domains of objects and rituals of truth. The individual and the knowledge that may be gained of him belong to this production" (p. 194). That is, the individual is constituted (or produced) within power relations and this production is ongoing throughout time. Foucault (1994) argues against the "absolute position of the subject" (p. 3), arguing, instead, that subjects are continually constituted and reconstituted by history. In addition to producing and constituting subjects over time, power also constitutes knowledge, constraining what is possible to know, what is accepted as knowledge, and constituting new knowledge forms. In his discussion of institutions, Foucault (1979) notes that defining the boundaries of the problem gives rise to specialized and elite knowledge. For example, in examining prison and mental hospitals, Foucault (1979) argues that elite bodies of specialized knowledge–disciplines like criminology and psychology–are created to define and address identified problems like delinquency and mental illness. The knowledge produced within these discourses limits what can be known about the individuals constituted as subjects. In our discussion, power shapes transition, creating subjects (e.g., student/ worker, student support professionals) and specialized knowledge areas (e.g., research on effective interventions to promote successful transition) that define and limit our understanding.

In describing the connection between power and knowledge, Foucault (1994) states:

> It is not natural for nature to be known. Thus, between the instincts and knowledge, one finds not a continuity but, rather, a relation of struggle, domination, servitude, settlement. In the same way, there can be no relation of natural continuity between knowledge and the things that knowledge must know. There can only be a relation of violence, domination, power, and force, a relation of violation. (p. 9)

Here, Foucault articulates the role of power in the creation of knowledge. There is no natural connection between "knowledge and the things that knowledge must know"; this relationship is determined by discursive arrangements that produce certain practices and forms of power-knowledge. When practices and constituting forms of power-knowledge are accepted as unquestionable or inevitable, they produce subjects and discourse that maintain these arrangements. Returning to the example of the prison, when prison is the accepted response to crime, specific subjects—the prisoner, guard, warden—are constituted within a discourse—criminology, penal studies—that produces and maintains these power arrangements as natural.

Foucault (1994) moves away from the individual subject as the "central core of all knowledge", recognizing that the subject and knowledge itself are produced through power relations (p.

3). The discursive arrangements that produce subjects, knowledge, and what is possible to know and do (specific practices) are powerful, constraining individual action or behaviour. As knowledge is created about what is good and bad (criminal, deviant, sick, abnormal, etc.) and power is exercised over those who do not conform to conceptualizations of 'good' (e.g., institutionalization, imprisonment, punishment, etc.), subjects self-govern and monitor their own conduct. Individuals have become subjects of normalization through mechanisms that are discursive in creating subjects that unconsciously discipline themselves (Foucault, 1979, p. 308).

In discussing Foucault's concepts of power, St. Pierre (2000) notes that although individuals internalize expectations that can lead to 'self-governing', power is a productive and relational force that can also be modified or reversed (p. 490). That is, power operates in relation, and is dynamic; so, while people may abide by norms and social expectations, power may be modified or reversed in forms of resistance to these norms and expectations. St. Pierre (2000) further explains that the presence of power elucidates freedom; power relations exist where there is "a certain degree of freedom on both sides" (p. 490). "Power is productive and can be found in the effects of liberty as well as in the effects of domination" (St. Pierre, 2000, p. 491). The fact that power demonstrates freedom and domination is important in understanding resistance to neoliberal discourses, which is my concern in this chapter. As power highlights the presence of freedom, and power is everywhere, resistance is always possible; resistance is an effect of a power relation. Therefore, although individuals are constituted within discursive arrangements that are produced through relations of power-knowledge, there is always the opportunity for resistance. Foucault (1994) argues that resistance "is a question of analyzing a 'regime of practices'; practices being understood here as places where what is said and what is done, rules imposed and reasons given, the planned and the taken-for-granted meet and interconnect" (p. 225). So, rather than accepting and internalizing conceptualizations of 'good' and 'normal' as inevitable, resistance involves examining and deconstructing concepts of good and normal to show how these practices are legitimized. This is the core of Foucault's work–to question and deconstruct taken-for-granted practices—and his analyses demonstrate the importance of, and possibility for, resistance. That is, Foucault emphasizes the importance of resisting, through question and critique, practices that are accepted as natural and inevitable. By making visible the relationship between power-knowledge, accepted practices, and the construction of subjects and material-discursive arrangements, Foucault creates space for resistance and new ideas of what could be.

While resistance is integral to Foucault's concepts, he does not seek to "dictate 'what is to be done'" (Foucault, 1994, p. 236). Instead, he sees the deconstruction and analysis of practices and techniques in their multiplicity (polymorphisms) of arrangements as a form of critique, of resistance. "Critique doesn't have to be the premise of a deduction that concludes, 'this, then, is what needs to be done.' It should be an instrument of those who fight, those who resist and refuse what is." (Foucault, 1994, p. 236). So, while Foucault articulates the need for critique, for resistance, and for refusing what is, he does not offer strategies of resistance and discounts the utility of prescriptive statements of what should be done (Foucault, 1994). This allows for generative resistance where the focus is on opening up new possibilities of what could be, rather than simply "refus(ing) what is" (Foucault, 1994, p. 236). Through this perspective of continual deconstruction, I explore the participants' experience of transition–their construction as subjects, the power relations that configure them, and their experiences of and capacities for resistance. Exploring how participants

63

navigate neoliberal constructions of themselves allows for a critical examination of the taken for granted and assumed to be inevitable aspects of education, transition, and work.

Resisting Neoliberal Definitions of "Success"

In this section, I put Foucault's concept of power to work to show how some of the participants deconstructed social mobility expectations and practices, questioning their origin, and resisting neoliberal conceptualizations of success as natural and inevitable.

As noted above, participants discussed the pressures they feel in comparing themselves to and competing with others (i.e., family and friends) in relation to their financial success; for example, having a house, obtaining a well-paying job, starting an RRSP. They felt the need to get somewhere fast, although they were unsure of their destination or found that the finish line kept changing. They discussed their educational, relational, and life experiences in an instrumental way in relation to the overarching goal of financial success; they asked how their experiences contribute to or detract from their concept of financial or material success. This is demonstrated in detail in discussing the participants' experience with the pressures to succeed; for example, both Matthew and Elizabeth analyzed their educational decisions regarding whether they are "worth it" financially. The participants described those experiences that do not directly contribute to financial success as a waste of time. For example, both Carolyn and Hannah loved their involvement in international social service work and felt it was one of the best experiences of their lives, yet both were wary of engaging in future international projects because it could put them behind where they want to be in relation to financial success and stability. They seem to moderate their internal desires and expectations with external pressures that are constraining their options. They self-govern to meet the social expectations they feel are placed upon them, reinforcing and reproducing neoliberal values of competition and success.

However, while the participants described the pressure they feel to compete and demonstrate material success, some participants also recognized their ability to resist this pressure and to think about what else may be possible. Carolyn, Hannah, and Alison discussed the need to step back from these powerful messages of where one should be (i.e., financially, socially, etc.). They described an active process whereby they make a choice not to buy into the externalized neoliberal pressures placed upon them (constructing them), and they stop themselves when they get caught up in the feeling of not being enough. Carolyn explained:

> But then I stop and think—for what? What am I not seeing right now? It is that inner dialogue. You can so easily get caught up in the idea of wasted time and get sad about it. Or you can see time not as a waste but as what makes me who I am. It would be a waste to feel like my life was a waste of time. I'm trying to figure this out for myself. If I can't learn how to stop and enjoy what's around me and who I am now—imperfections and all—then I am just wasting time trying to prove myself to someone else or myself. Not valuing the time I do have. Trying to see the world like that makes for a much more productive and happy life. It is super hard. Super challenging. That's the message—even growing up as a low-income immigrant kid—I wasn't white enough, Korean enough, Canadian enough. Never enough. Then growing up, I am reteaching myself to talk to myself in a way that's empowering.

For Carolyn, comparing herself to others resulted in a feeling of never being enough. Rather than trying to compete, she stated that she actively stops and reflects on how she is using her time. She reframed the idea of "wasted time" (i.e., time spent on activities and experiences that do not directly contribute to overall goals of financial success) to recognize that the time she has invested in different experiences has made her who she is today. Carolyn discussed the need to value who she is and to honour where she is on her own life trajectory. She focused on gratitude—on recognizing what she does have, rather than focusing on what she is lacking. However, this is not an easy perspective to hold onto. The default position seems to be to fall back into competition, comparison, and feeling not enough:

> I feel competitive, but then I reflect on these thoughts and learn how to be grateful. Working in this field is incredibly humbling. People are dealt really shitty hands. And you forget to see how much you've been given. I get to eat three times a day. I have people who love me and I love people. Still, it is a real struggle to remember, be thankful, and try to maintain balance. It is easy to slip into that competitive mindset without even being conscious of it. I want to be genuinely happy for others and be content with where I am currently while still growing. That is the ultimate dream.

In this part of our discussion, Carolyn compared herself to the people she works with, who are "dealt really shitty hands". This, in contrast to comparisons to "successful" friends and family members earlier, helps Carolyn reframe her experience and be grateful for what she has. She continues to navigate this binary between self/other to help determine her own position—what she *should* have and what she *should* be. In this way, Carolyn is enacting reflective skills associated with being a social service worker to disrupt some of the expectations involved in transitioning into the social service work field.

Hannah, who enhances inclusivity in childcare settings, felt uncertainty about her work and future. She, like Carolyn, explained that she has been working on reframing her uncertainty; she noted that she is recognizing what she has and feeling grateful and, in doing so, has a renewed sense of peace. She explained that she was feeling pressure to figure out what to do next (in terms of education and career), but that she has moved beyond that feeling and is trying to be consciously happy:

> That sense of peace has come in talking through this with a lot of people in my support system. Family and friends. Many people have reassured me that I am in a good place—you are 24, you work in a good agency, have a Bachelor's degree, etc. Again, I think I've been focusing on being consciously happy because I don't want to miss it and always be focusing on the next thing. So I feel more fulfilled.

Hannah discusses intentionally reframing her experience and looking to others to determine if she is where she *should* be. She similarly navigates the binary between self/others and feels reassured by others—family and friends—who tell her that she is "in a good place"; that is, she is reassured that she is enough by those around her. In addition to reassurance from others, Hannah also focuses on "being consciously happy"; Hannah is drawing on a different ideology—being present, practicing gratitude—to resist neoliberalism.

Alison recognized that external pressures and messages of 'not being enough' construct her, even when her values are inconsistent with the dominant neoliberal values idealized socially (e.g., consumption, financial success, competition, etc.). Here she reframed what she has been able to do, how she has succeeded, by her own benchmarks of what is valuable:

> I am able to pay my bills every month and I don't carry a credit card debt so that is the most exciting thing I can say about where I am at. That comes with having been on my own at a very young age and learning to balance that. It all comes back into a capitalist market economy and where you ought to be

within that, and that dictates how you interact with every other social institution from the work you do, to being in school, to everything. It is all embedded in that. And I've consciously resisted that my whole life. Funny that even if I don't place value within any of that, I've still very much internalized those messages. There are dominant discourses that I may not believe in but very much influence me. Being aware of that and not letting it get the better of me is very important. Even within my own values, none of this is important to me but I make sense of myself also through how others see me. So, my identity isn't just internal—it is also relational. And if I am seen as not quite getting it right, it is going to have a negative effect on me. I recognize that most of those things that I feel like I'm failing at adulting are not values that are mine anyway, so I'm like, wait, that's not my value, never mind. It comes back to resistance. Recognizing that it is an aspect of the system that I've never appreciated anyway, so I don't need to worry about that. So when those feelings do come up, it is questioning whether I feel like I am failing myself or if that is something that someone else expects of me. How many expectations have we all built up about ourselves that may not be meaningful to us at all , and we are totally taking for granted? What is frustrating about that for me is trying to decide whether something is my own value or is it something implicit from my family or society. I'm 30. I've done a lot of pretty great things in my life. I'm proud of where I am. But I forget that all the time.

Alison's discussion highlighted the distinction (often comparison) between self/other and how one navigates internal and external pressures and expectations. She recognized that her identity is "also relational", so that how she views herself (as 'enough', as an 'adult', as 'successful') is influenced by how others view her. When others do not see her as successful, this negatively influences her self-concept, even when she does not share these values. As with Carolyn and Hannah's intentional reframing above, Alison stated that she actively resists external expectations and tries to determine her own values and expectations. She described this as actually stopping the process—"I'm like, wait, that's not my value"—and assessing whether the values she holds are truly her own or are societal values that she has internalized without critical thought. Although Alison explicitly differentiated between her "own values" and what others expect of her, she is constituted by discourse within Foucault's conceptualization, even if this discourse is disruptive to neoliberalism. Alison, Carolyn, and Hannah also discussed the importance of knowing themselves—listening to and questioning themselves to determine what they think, feel, know, and do. Resistance then involves drawing upon other discourses that question, deconstruct, and speak back to the dominant neoliberal discourse.

These narratives suggest that Alison, Carolyn, and Hannah constantly construct and reconstruct themselves in an incomplete process, where they are open to new formations (St. Pierre, 2000). They are navigating and disrupting a series of binaries—self/other, internal/external, enough/not enough—throughout their transition. At times, they actively resist the internalized and external messages of competition and success by stopping, re-evaluating those messages, and reframing their own experiences within discourses of gratitude and intentional happiness. They are redefining what it means to have and be 'enough' in a globalized, capitalist society, which can be disruptive and generative within that society.

Power, Resistance, and Transition

In their ongoing disruption of self/other, internal/external, and enough/not enough, the participants' narratives demonstrated how power works through them. They are not powerless and oppressed by neoliberal ideology and social mobility discourse. Neoliberal ideology and social mobility discourse are powerful and harmful in participants' lives, but participants intentionally draw on other discourses to disrupt the inevitability of neoliberalism and provide new possibilities for living. Power flows through the participants in relation to others. The participants, in a Foucauldian sense, do not hold power as individuals but exercise power in different ways, in varied entanglements, situations, and experiences. The participants are constituted through the power-knowledge discourses that are constraining them. They have internalized the importance of normative ideas of being 'enough' and 'success' but are using elements of their education and life experiences (e.g., self-reflection, strength-based practice, reframing) to critique these ideas. The participants do not accept the way things are or take for granted the inevitability of current definitions of 'success'. Instead, they have questioned their perspectives and values and contextualized their experience within a broader social narrative. This critique is a form of resistance that is consistent with Foucault's conceptualization of power and of resistance as a deconstruction of dominant practices and discourses. This resistance is also consistent with the literature that finds that students tend to resist internalizing the messages of neoliberal ideology when they recognize the promise of a "good life" (Cairns, 2013)–gaining economic and social mobility through hard work, higher education, and employment–is inconsistent with their lived experiences (Allen et al., 2013; Hull, 1993; Hull & Zacher, 2007; Valadez, 2000).

Reading the participants' experiences through Foucault's concepts provides a different perspective of the transition to social service work. Rather than viewing the experiences of participants as moving seamlessly and in a linear direction from school to work, from being a student to becoming a successful, professional adult, a Foucauldian analysis suggests that participants continually navigate neoliberal expectations and question the promise of a 'good life' after post-secondary. The process of internalizing neoliberal ideals in school and work is more nuanced and complex than simply acceptance/rejection, as participants navigate who they are, what their role is in the field of social service work, and what they value. The participants, as new social service workers, critique ideas of competition and meritocracy, critically reflecting upon and questioning these ideals, and are challenged not to default back into this dominant discourse. The influence of neoliberal ideology that colours school and work exerts pressure throughout the transition, and the participants discussed resistance and critique as an active, intentional process. Foucault's conceptualization of power allows for an interconnected view of power relations that moves beyond the individual, instead focusing on on social and discursive arrangements. In addition, thinking with Foucault demonstrates transition as an ongoing process that students/workers continually navigate. The power that flows in relationships has meaningful implications for social service work and for education as these are relational fields involving power differentials (e.g., teacher/student, worker/client); the idea of power flowing in relation, rather than being held by an individual, has the potential to alter relational work.

In a practical sense, this means that power flows through social service workers as they actively critique the dominant ideal of a 'good life'; instead of working towards neoliberal goals, social service workers can help those they serve to identify what is important and meaningful to them, in their own lives. Social service workers recognize that not everyone is afforded the same privileges and can empathize with each unique individual, working on creating the vision of the life that the person served wants for themselves. The power relationship is not one of the 'worker' holding power over the 'client', or of the worker trying to empower the client. In-

71

stead, power flows through their relationship and in relation to the agencies and institutions within which they operate. Social service workers can advocate for those they work with, arguing against the concept of meritocracy and competition, and promoting understanding of intersecting vulnerabilities. Working within agencies that must demonstrate effectiveness and efficiency to funding agents, social service workers can stop and critically question the technocratic requirements of their role. Power flows through them as they navigate the tensions between these requirements and the needs of the people they serve.

Following Ideas of 'Not Enough'

The participants' narratives highlight the tensions that exist as they transition through neoliberal institutions (post-secondary to the labour market) and are challenged by societal views of success. Their narratives highlight that while resistance is possible, participants' internalized views of neoliberal measures of success led to questioning themselves and their trajectories. So, while Foucault's conceptualization of power offers a framework for the resistance demonstrated in the participants' narratives, this concept does not allow for exploration of the feelings of 'not enough' that emerged. An affective intensity of 'enoughness' seemed to pervade the participants' discussions of navigating neoliberal pressures and expectations in transitioning from post-secondary education to working in the social service field. I felt, in hearing, reading, and analyzing our conversations: the pressure to be, and to feel, *enough* relative to their position in society, but also in their professional role in helping marginalized people. That intensity resounded with me in my experience in social service work and academia and led to further examination of my questions about how participants' identities are enacted differently as 'students' and 'workers'. How do participants take on the identity of a social service worker? What shapes their identities? Is there a feeling of 'enough' in taking on this identity? In the following chapter, I draw on Butler's concept of performativity to explore the participants' experiences of their identity as social service workers. This analysis builds on Foucault's concept of power, as power flows in the construction of participants as social service workers but allows for a more nuanced understanding of how the participants see themselves as they transition into social service workers.

References

Allen, K., Quinn, J., Hollingworth, S., & Rose, A. (2013). Becoming employable students and 'ideal' creative workers: exclusion and inequality in higher education work placements. *British Journal of Sociology of Education, 34*(3), 431-452. doi: 10.1080/01425692.2012.714249

Cairns, K. (2013). The subject of neoliberal affects: Rural youth envision their futures. *The Canadian Geographer, 57*(3), 337-344. doi: 10.1111/cag.12012

Foucault, M. (1979). *Discipline and punish: The birth of the prison.* (A. Sheridan, Trans.). Vintage.

Foucault, M. (1994). *Michel Foucault: Power.* (R. Hurley, Trans.). J. D. Faubion (Ed.). The New Press.

Hull, G. A. (1993). Critical literacy and beyond: Lessons learned from students and workers in a vocational program and on the job. *Anthropology and Education Quarterly, 24*(4), 373-396. https://www-jstor-org.proxy.lib.sfu.ca/stable/3195937

Hull, G., & Zacher, J. (2007). Enacting identities: An ethnography of a job training program. *International Journal of Theory and Research, 7*(1), 71-102. doi: 10.1080/15283480701319708

Nairn, K., Higgins, J., & Sligo, J. (2012). *Children of Rogernomics: A neoliberal generation leaves school.* Otago University Press.

St. Pierre, E. A. (2000). Post-structural feminism in education: An overview. *International Journal of Qualitative Studies in Education, 13*(5), 477-515. doi: 10.1080/09518390050156422

Valadez, J. R. (2000). Searching for a path out of poverty: Exploring the achievement ideology of a rural community college. *Adult Education Quarterly, 50*(3), 212-230. https://doi-org.proxy.lib.sfu.ca/10.1177/07417130022087017

Chapter 5

"Never Enough"—Performing as Social Service Worker

While examining the conversations I had with the social service workers through Foucault's concept of power, questions about how the participants took up their role and identity in social service practice emerged. While thinking with *power* provided a framework for resistance to neoliberal ideology, the analysis (in Chapter 4) raised additional questions about identity, self-concept, and the participants feeling that they were not 'enough'.

Throughout their experiences of resisting neoliberal ideology, participants wrestled with feelings of 'enoughness' by asking, "Am I enough?". The idea of enoughness prompted me to further explore the participants' identities and how they come to see themselves as social service workers. This concept led me to examine how participants see, know, and describe themselves as 'students' and 'workers' and how they enact various identities across social, political, and institutional contexts. In the present chapter, I discuss how participants understand their role as social service workers and how they assess themselves against these expectations. As articulated by Judith Butler (1999), I use the concept of performativity to examine participants' ongoing negotiation of the social service role and related feelings of enoughness. Thinking with Butler's concept of performativity builds upon my thinking with Foucault; power flows through participants as they navigate the conflicting values of social service work and neoliberal ideology, finding ways to resist and explore different ways of living. Power does not only constrain the construction of the participants as social service workers; it also works through them in their performance of social service worker identities.

Moving beyond the neoliberal definitions of success, I examine how the participants continually navigate conflicting values as they transition into being social service workers. I use the concept of performativity, building upon Foucault's concept of power, to analyze the work social service workers do to construct and become recognized in their professional roles. I discuss the relationship between performing an identity and being recognized and acknowledged by others. I also explore how participants resist the construct of the ideal social service worker, reconstituting and resignifying themselves and their professional role.

Experiences of the 'Ideal' Social Service Worker

Transitioning into the field, workers develop their new identity as social service workers. In discussing their identity, several participants said they were unclear about what a social service worker is or does or how to manage conflicting expectations within the role. As new practitioners in social services, the participants are attempting to master a role "for which they have little or no first-hand knowledge" (Davies, 2006, p. 433). The role of 'social service worker' is unstable and unattainable, yet the participants continuously perform and strive for this undefined ideal. As demonstrated in the following discussion, the 'ideal' social service worker is a complex arrangement of responsibilities and expectations enacted in relationship with various stakeholders. In other words, the ideal social service worker is many things to many different people, often creating tensions between conflicting positions.

The participants I spoke to discussed navigating their identities; participants are "still figuring it out", as participant Carolyn explained. In our first interview, Carolyn was only two months into her current position but had worked in other social service positions and had considerable international experience doing relational work. Despite her experience, Carolyn felt unsure about herself in her role. During our second interview, we first reflected together on issues that emerged in the first interview and reviewed the narrative summary. At this point, Carolyn shared feelings of uncertainty and ambivalence, explaining: "[The narrative] seems to show some ambivalence about what my future will hold and shows that I still have a lot of questions—Where will I go? What does it mean to be a professional? I still have a lot of those questions." She later went on to elaborate on that ambivalence, explaining, "I am a little bit in-between". In this conversation, Carolyn voiced a desire to be constructed as a professional, but she was not yet sure what that meant and was feeling "in-between" the role of student and the role of worker. As the participants are constructed as social service workers, they are also recognized as capable, empathic, relational practitioners. A recognition of being enough is a relational process between the participants, the persons served, colleagues, and others; through these relationships, the participants are constructed as social service workers. Feeling "in-between" student/worker challenges how Carolyn may be recognized by others and influences her feelings of being enough.

Hannah, Carolyn, and Matthew discussed their uncertainty about being enough in their role as social service workers. This uncertainty presented as participants questioned whether they were selfless, passionate, or competent enough to perform their jobs. For example, Hannah was unsure of the expectations of her role and questioned whether she was "selfless enough" or "passionate enough", seeing these characteristics as necessary for social service work. Hannah noted she received "mixed messages" throughout her education; she remembered guest speakers presenting conflicting information about what was required as a social service worker:

> There were mixed messages (in the degree program) about the importance of self-care and preventing burnout while at the same time saying you had to give it your all, and if a family called in the middle of the night, you answered. I question if I am selfless enough to do this work. I wonder if I am passionate enough about what I do.

Hannah was unclear about what is expected from the ideal, professional social service worker. From Hannah's description, there may be varied expectations in different contexts (e.g., education, agencies with different mandates, etc.) that are not clearly articulated or may, in fact, be contradictory; for example, students are being taught to be selfless yet to also prioritize self-care. Hannah went on to explain that as she gained experience in her role, she struggled to balance her needs and the needs of those she served in a way that fit for her. This was an ongoing challenge in defining herself in her work and in being recognized as a good social service worker; Hannah stated that colleagues often commented on her ability to set time for herself, that was presented as a compliment, but that she received more as a "backhanded" commentary that Hannah was not prioritizing the needs of those she works with.

Carolyn expressed similar concerns during her transition into social service work. She explained that when she first came into the field, she worked for approximately one year with a very complex population—those who face the most significant and intersecting challenges. Here Carolyn questioned if social service work was a good fit; as she explained, she had a "humbling realization that this may not be for me". In fact, Carolyn left social service work for two years and had only just recently returned to her position at the time of the interview. Although she expressed that her current position had a "steep learning curve", she kept telling herself she could do it. Carolyn's hiatus from social service work and her affirming self-talk demonstrate how important feeling competent and enough are in this work. Carolyn's self-talk and Hannah's example of balancing her personal and professional lives highlight the subjectivity involved in social service work. As social service workers bring themselves into their relational practice, they navigate and perform the role in a way that fits for them.

Matthew also questioned his competence within his role. He senses the expectation to be proficient, to work quickly, to be independent, and he is struggling to learn it all:

> I don't feel comfortable with things that I haven't done in a while—I feel really new. What if something happens and I have to write up paperwork? It is a busy, busy place, and you can't take forever to write up paperwork. You have to be proficient. Most of the people I work with will show me things, so I learn while I'm there, but I'm definitely new. My last shift was a day shift at a slower shelter, and I learned a lot about computer work. I'm sensitive that I haven't learned as much as I could or should. My willingness is there. I just need more opportunities and maybe that will come in time.

For Matthew, being 'enough' is connected to completing paperwork on the computer, which is an increasingly important task and responsibility in social service work. It is interesting that Hannah, Elizabeth, and Alison also discussed the importance of paperwork and the struggle to adequately represent their work in writing to supervisors, and, ultimately, funding agents. There is an apparent tension between engaging in relational work and writing about this work in a way that fits with the measures demanded by funders and the accountability culture of neoliberalism. I analyze this tension further in the upcoming section on "Resisting the 'Ideal Social Service Worker'".

While Hannah, Carolyn, and Matthew questioned their capacity to meet the expectations of the 'ideal' social service worker, Elizabeth discussed her feelings of enoughness in relation to her work being recognized by others. Elizabeth explained that she felt her work matters and that she has a meaningful impact on the people she works with in her role, but that she had difficulty communicating what she does with people in a way that meaningfully represents the work. She noted that people outside of the field seem to misunderstand or downplay the therapeutic aspect of her work and that her work is minimized by those who don't understand. She discussed how people outside of the field may see her work in terms of —"oh, you just...". In attempting to be recognized as a competent, effective, and professional social service worker, Elizabeth felt her work could be dismissed as, "oh, you just watch TV with clients", overlooking the complexity of relational work with (in Elizabeth's case) people with significant mental health challenges living independently. Elizabeth went on to explain that people in the field also tend to minimize their own work:

> Even hearing people say, I'm *just* a...What value do you place on what you do and how you explain it? There is a lot that rides on that. If you want people to have an accurate view of what you do, and it may be different depending upon who you are talking to, how you explain it could be very different. People in the field may know the agency or the type of work where others in other fields wouldn't. And the role and field fluctuate and change so often.

To Elizabeth, social service workers must articulate their role and the value of their role clearly, so the work is legitimized and recognized by others. She notes that the field of social service work is dynamic and continually changing in terms of accepted and supported approaches to the work (Elizabeth used the example of moving to more client-driven recovery models of service). These changes may not be well understood outside of the field. The subtle complexity of social service work may result in the work going unrecognized.

When in a place of not knowing or uncertainty, participants seem to define themselves in relation to what they are not. For example, although Carolyn stated that she was unsure and in-between, she was able to resist certain constructions of herself as a social service worker. She spoke about her previous work experience, where she felt like she was only acting as a 'gatekeeper' for shelter services. She explained this further:

> When I was discussing my experience at my last job, I meant that I was the person who allows people access to service or decides to discharge people but I had minimal relationships with the people who were being served. I felt like it didn't build on my relational skills. It was not complex. I was just tasked with discharging clients, and I didn't enjoy being that door. I wasn't interested in that role.

In this excerpt, while Carolyn was not yet clear on what it means to be constructed as a social service worker, she knew she did not want to be in a position where her primary responsibility was determining who receives or does not receive service. In the example she described, Carolyn was working with highly vulnerable women with multiple barriers; in very real ways, those who were discharged or denied service were at very high risk for violence, trauma, and death. She left that position, choosing not to submit to the expectation that she become a 'gatekeeper' for service. She did not identify with this more technocratic role, emphasizing the need to be relational—to build meaningful relationships with the people being served—as a defining aspect of her working identity. Seeing this as an example of resistance to identifying as an ideal social service worker, I turn to Butler's conceptualization of performativity to understand how participants negotiated varied, and sometimes contradictory, expectations of being a social service worker. I examine how they aligned with their role and how they worked from within the role to re-inscribe who and what a social service worker should be. I think of transition as a performance, analyzing the participants' performances of an ideal social service worker to demonstrate how participants' "identities get done and undone" as they perform multiple and dynamic subjectivities (Jackson & Mazzei, 2012, p. 67).

Butler's Conceptualization of Performativity

Butler deconstructs identity as a stable and essential characteristic of an individual, arguing that identities are repetitive acts that are performed in attempts to meet an idealized norm. As a feminist philosopher, Judith Butler critiques the foundations of feminism by troubling what it means to be a 'woman'. If feminism is meant to provide a voice for women, she asks, what constitutes a 'woman'? Butler (1999) troubles the idea that there is a defining essence of womanhood. Instead, she proposes that bodies are continually produced and reproduced within culture; identities such as gender are created through repetitive performances. Butler (1999) notes that "gender ought not to be construed as a stable identity or locus of agency from which various acts follow; rather, gender is an identity tenuously constituted in time, instituted in an exterior space through a stylized repetition of acts" (p. 179). In other words, identity is not produced by an internal essence but through a performance which consists of the repetition of acts, gestures, and enactments (Butler, 1999).

Viable and recognizable roles or identities are culturally

formed, and individuals attempt to perform these idealized roles. Yet, actors fall short of these idealized expectations, which are formed through power relations involving culture, discourse, and material arrangements. To relate this back to gender, there are cultural expectations related to being a 'man' or 'woman'. These normative expressions of gender (i.e., masculinity/femininity) determine what is possible. While individuals may perform as a man or as a woman, the idealized expectation of manhood or womanhood cannot be achieved. As each individual "never quite inhabit(s) the ideal s/he is compelled to approximate" (Butler, 1999, p. 231), s/he continues performing towards this expectation. This repetition constructs the norms as natural and inevitable and constructs the individual (subject) as gendered; it is through their repetitive performance that the subject expresses a recognizable gender and reinforces gender norms as natural. Those who do not perform according to these norms are informally and formally disciplined through a variety of measures.

> Gender is, thus, a construction that regularly conceals its genesis; the tacit collective agreement to perform, produce, and sustain discrete and polar genders as cultural fictions is obscured by the credibility of those productions— and the punishments that attend not agreeing to believe in them; the construction "compels" our belief in its necessity and naturalness. (Butler, 1999, p. 178)

In this excerpt, Butler (1999) explains that "discrete and polar genders" are constructed, reproduced, and sustained through performance and through the punishment of those who do not subscribe to binary gender. In other words, a subject is recognized through their performance which approximates the idealized norm. Although no one will actualize the ideal, always falling short of expectations, some subjects are recognized through their repetitive performance. Those who live outside of the idealized norm, or who are subversive in their performance, may be marked by precarity, including increased risk of poverty, injury, disease, violence, and death (Butler, 2009). Those outside of what is deemed acceptable are not recognizable and subsequently not worthy subjects. For Butler (2009), this is a political process whereby individuals perpetuate norms to gain recognition but simultaneously discard others to precarity. Butler examines the socially produced subject, who is constituted and constrained through power relations, and argues that performativity determines who is "eligible for recognition"; that is, performativity is connected to who counts and doesn't count as subjects (Butler, 2009, p. iv). As she explains:

> Performativity is a process that implies being acted on in ways we do not always fully understand, and of acting, in politically consequential ways. Performativity has everything to do with "who" can become produced as a recognizable subject, a subject who is living, whose life is worth sheltering and whose life, when lost, would be worthy of mourning. Precarious life characterizes such lives who do not qualify as recognizable, readable, or grievable. (Butler, 2009, p. xii- xiii)

Performativity is thus not merely a performance, but a process of subjectification; one is constituted as a subject through the repetition of a performative doing. That is, a subject is recognized through their performance; the subject comes into being by closely approximating the ideal category. Drawing on both Butler and Foucault, Davies (2006) explains that this process of becoming a subject, involves simultaneously both mastery and submission. That is, a subject is constituted in relationship to others; this relationship is marked by power. Power relations shape the subject in that the subject submits to the normative expectations of the prevailing material-discursive arrangements. As the subject seeks to master these expectations, these arrangements are reiterated and reproduced, and are seen as natural and inevitable. As the subject masters normative expectations, they may see themselves as capable, autonomous, and powerful; however, their construction is dependent upon their submission to the norms that determine what they can become. In her discussion of recognition and precarity, Butler (2004) explains the constraints that limit how a subject may be constructed:

> What counts as a person? ... What qualifies as a citizen? Whose world is legitimated as real? ... advance for me? By what norms am I constrained as I begin to ask what I may become? And what happens when I begin to become that for which there is no place within the given regime of truth? (p. 58)

Performativity and precarity are meaningful concepts for examining social services. The most apparent demonstration of these concepts is in how people within the social service system—individuals facing significant challenges, including trauma, homelessness, addiction, mental health concerns, criminal justice involvement, systematic racism, and the effects of colonization—are discarded to precarity. Due to the complex and often intersecting challenges these people face, they do not meet (are unable to meet?) societal expectations of appropriate subject positions. As they are not performing according to societal expectations, they are not recognized as subjects whose lives are worth sheltering; instead, they are often dehumanized and deemed unworthy.

Social service workers are also performing towards the ideal expression of their role. The participants discussed trying to perform an ideal subject position (i.e., the ideal social service worker) while being unclear on what that role entails. So, while social service workers engage with people discarded to precarity, the workers themselves are also living precarious lives. Social service workers often live outside of the idealized norm—including outside of neoliberal definitions of 'success'.

They face tenuous employment (e.g., contracts, part-time work, lack of benefits) and living environments, transience, and a lack of recognition in the legitimacy of their work because the people with whom they work are not recognized as legitimate subjects. Some examples of this precarity are evident in Chapter 4, where the participants discussed their experiences of conflicting and often unrealistic pressures to succeed.

The concept of performativity clarifies that the identities of 'student' and 'worker' are not stable characteristics but ongoing performances. Butler's conceptualization of performativity retheorizes identity, not as fixed, stable, and knowable, but as a dynamic performance within social, historical, and cultural contexts. Identity is constituted, in relation to power, within discursive and material arrangements, and contextualized by culture and history. As such, identity is both being constituted by these factors, while simultaneously being altered and undone as the factors themselves are constantly changing; I explore these factors in relation to the participants' narratives in the next section. Performativity also "produces the space of conflicting subjectivities" (Jackson, 2004, p. 675). That is, recognizing identity as performance allows for "fluid" and "contradictory" understandings of self that are relational (Jackson, 2004, p. 673); conflicting aspects of identity can be performed in different times, spaces, and with different people. While identities are shaped by power and situated in discourse, they are always "open for reconfiguration" (Jackson, 2004, p. 674). As Jackson (2004) explains, "there is always space for reworking and resisting" (p. 675). Therefore, performativity can be subversive, allowing subjects to critique and deconstruct the identity categories to which they belong; I will explore these potentialities as I examine the participants' experiences performing social service worker.

Resisting the 'Ideal' Social Service Worker

While subjects are constituted through performative acts that are constrained by discursive arrangements and power relations, the ongoing process of performance creates space for challenge and resistance. In this section, I examine how participants re-signified what it meant to demonstrate mastery of their social service worker role, altering their perception of the 'ideal' worker. The participants' dynamic definition of mastery, while beneficial to relational work with the people they serve, is in tension with neoliberal managerial expectations. This tension can jeopardize the recognition of participants as professionals, resulting in precarity.

Hannah, Alison, and Carolyn discussed a shift in their understanding of an ideal social service worker and their relationship to those they serve. For example, Hannah discussed "expertise" as an element of her work that is consistent with mastery. She explained that she often felt she was not taken seriously in her work due to her age, and I asked her about whether having her expertise recognized was important to her. Hannah explained that she wants to demonstrate mastery, or expertise, but that it is not necessary in her role:

> I like how you focused on the importance of expertise. That may be a personal thing for me. That may be me searching to be really good at something. Or wanting to have all the answers because I'm new. It is important to me, but isn't really important to the job. It is important to just be present and give it your all.

Hannah does not need to know everything or be considered an expert. Mastery, for her, may involve being present and engaged with the people she serves. The performance of social service work, in Hannah's context, does not require "having all the answers"; instead, expertise could reflect being present and putting the needs of those you serve before one's own. Hannah's approach transgresses a dominant view of social service work whereby the social service worker is educated, equipped, and seen as an expert that can intervene with a 'client' to promote positive outcomes. Hannah developed from "wanting to have all the answers" to recognizing the importance of being present with the people she works with.

In keeping with Hannah's description of needing to be present and engaged, Alison recognized that mastering her role does not involve "fixing" anyone. Within the context of her agency and the mandate she works within (which is a drop-in centre for youth with addiction, mental health, and/or homelessness operating from a harm reduction approach), she sees how power operates on her and through her and through the young people with whom she works, and through the very terrain of addiction and homelessness. She stated that "power is always operating. I'm not an expert of their life and their context. I go into my work as server, not expert." Alison recognized the power differential inherent in her relationship with the young people she works with and the structural constraints that intersect for them, and she tries to approach her relational work as service. She went on to explain:

> I'm not expected to fix anyone. I really get to sit in that place of not knowing what the right answer is and I get to explore that with the youth on their own terms. That feels really good in comparison to intervention-based work.

Both Alison and Hannah, as new to social service, attempted to perform their new subject positions without fully understanding what a social service worker is and does. Their subjectification, or process of recognition, was to learn how to master the expectations of the field. While they submitted themselves to the expectations of the field, they were also aware of their own involvement in maintaining and reproducing power relations and were sensitive to power in navigating their performance as social service workers. Alison recognized that "power is always operating," and rather than attempt to take a position of authority and expertise, both Hannah and Alison recognized the need to be vulnerable, by being present to the dynamic needs of those they serve. As new workers in the field, Alison and Hannah (and the other participants) are seeking recognition as socially viable subjects. However, it is difficult for them to determine their own worth; they never quite know whether they are fulfilling the expectations of their role or effectively addressing the needs of those they serve. Hannah explained:

> We aren't able to measure our effectiveness. Our focus is on helping at-risk and vulnerable populations—you are never really going to know how you impacted someone. It has to come from a place of feeling confident. That you did the best you could. That you used an approach that is known to help most people. There isn't a lot of certainty.

While Hannah could not know if her work was effective, she articulated the need to feel confident in her approach and to know she had done her best. Rather than measure herself against the unattainable ideal of the social service worker, increased confidence and knowledge she has done her best in her work helped Hannah recognize her own worth. For Alison, not knowing provided some freedom, the freedom to be present and attend to the needs of those she serves, without evaluating her effectiveness by unrealistic and unattainable standards. Alison explained that mastery is letting go of the need to have all the answers; to remove the expectation of expertise:

> That mindset of not knowing takes the pressure off needing to have answers to huge structural and social problems that don't currently have answers. I work through the problem on

a case-by-case basis, in terms of where can I get a meal, and it makes it more tangible. School has a very grand focus on social justice, and it is humbling to recognize that making tea and checking in with someone while they watch cartoons is an act of social justice because no one else is checking in with them to see if they're okay. Recognizing that each youth is worthy of respect and dignity. I think it does make a difference. It is really just about seeing people and attending to them.

To Alison, mastery of her role involved addressing the immediate needs of the youth (providing resources for a meal, making tea, and checking in) rather than resolving huge social problems, like homelessness, addiction, and mental health. Her conception of good work emphasizes the material—a meal, a cup of tea, warm bodies, providing a safe physical space. This youth-centered approach may allow her to be recognized as a good social service worker by the people she serves as well as like-minded colleagues in the field. However, Alison noted later in our conversation that the public often does not recognize the importance of this type of work. She explained that "there is pressure on us, as professionals in the field, because we are looked at like—why aren't we fixing this? Why aren't we doing our job?" in relation to resolving social inequities and "fixing" homelessness, addiction, and other complex social issues. Alison is both recognized and not recognized as a 'good' worker, depending upon the different environments in which she circulates; this potential failure to be recognized in her role holds the potential for precarity for Alison. I explore the connection between participants' performances and precarity in greater detail below.

As Alison suggests above, she has been subjected to pressures to resolve social injustices that far exceed her direct work with young people. In the experiences of the participants, their work (and subsequently, themselves as viable subjects) can go unrecognized when there are contradictory views on what the work entails. For example, as seen above, Carolyn, Hannah, and Alison emphasize that 'good' social service workers are relational, present, and humble, acting from a place of service rather than authority or expertise. However, this subjectivity may not be recognized by agencies and/or funders who operate from a managerial perspective. As examined in Chapter 2, neoliberal ideology promotes a managerial perspective that emphasizes the measurement of predetermined outcomes, standardization, efficiency, and individual responsibility. Hannah articulately explained the disparity and tension between relational practice and outcome-focused service deliverables:

> I find everything so formal here. In our job, we need to spend 50% of our time in the community but also need to write reports and do all of our paperwork. It is formal, and you have to follow policies and protocol. Everything is documented, every communication written down, everything can be challenged. I am very relational but there is pressure to produce certain targets, goals, and outcomes. I feel like I have to sell something. And in a field where there is no right answer, and there is a lack of definitiveness, how do you justify what you are doing? There are so many politics here—the government gives us funds and tells us how to use them, but they are not social service workers; they don't have a child and youth care (CYC) background. They don't get it and we have to report to that. I didn't get how much that confines you and how much that shapes the field. It would be nice to have people who really get what the work is about writing policy so it can be more relational practice. In CYC, we learn about the importance of relational practice but it is not respected once you get out there—all that's respected, like in business or anything else—is output.

Hannah meets the requirement to justify her work through paperwork and reports, demonstrating that she is effective at her job by meeting specific targets, goals, and outcomes. This, she explained, is contradictory to relational practice, which is foundational in the teaching of social service work. Thus, she discussed experiencing a disconnect between the forms of mastery students are taught in their post-secondary education and what she experienced in the field. Being a 'good' social service worker means, to funders and policy makers, being effective and efficient. Consistent with neoliberal ideologies, failing to perform efficacy and efficiency, as demonstrated through paperwork and outcome reporting, is considered an individual failing. Hannah stated she was unaware how much funding expectations and requirements shape the field and would constrain her work. The policies and funding requirements shape Hannah as a subject within the conditions of her work.

Alison also discussed the tension between relational work with those she works with and the requirements of the agency mandate or funding agents:

> It is not that staff themselves are not trying to help and trying to have good relational practice. There is only so much they can do. When we are trying to meet the needs of the client, we still have to work within someone else' mandate, someone else's expectations, and we are still expected to toe the line. That moves the focus away from the client and onto what the funder needs. There is always a tension between doing what the client needs and doing what we, as an agency, have to do to show our numbers so we can continue to get funding so we can stay open, and try to help as many people as we can.

These narratives demonstrate the contested power relations involved in social service work. The participants discussed re-signifying their work as relational, re-casting expertise as the capacity to be present, humble, and engaged, rather than having all the answers. Through this altered performance, the participants are transgressing or resisting the 'ideal social service worker' and redefining what it means to do good, ethical work with clients. However, this relational work may not be recognized by supervisors or funding agents, who, consistent with neoliberal ideology, seek measurable and reportable outcomes demonstrating effectiveness and efficiency. The performance of the social service worker that Hannah, Alison, and Carolyn promote may also not be recognized by the public, who minimize the work done as, for example, "just watching TV with clients". As discussed by Alison, the public may see social service workers as responsible for resolving social inequities and injustice without understanding the complexity of these arrangements. This threatens social service workers being recognized as worthy and puts social service workers in a precarious position.

As social service workers, Hannah and Alison exercise power over those they serve. They communicated their awareness of this and approach their relationships with those they serve intentionally, in order to minimize power working through them in an oppressive way. Social service workers are, in turn, constrained and shaped by power within the agencies in which they work. They are supervised in a hierarchical system of accountability, which ultimately includes the funding agent of the agency. To be constructed as a good worker, the participants have to oscillate between subjectivities: being present and relational while also being able to articulately justify their work to supervisors and ultimately rationalize the existence of their program to funders. In the process of being recognized as viable subjects, social service workers need to be able to work across these different arrangements (i.e., relational practice and outcome-focused managerialism), shifting the way they perform their work. As they perform, the participants have the power to enact aspects of the social service worker role and to critique, deconstruct, and challenge that idealized identity from within.

Alison spoke explicitly about the need to re-signify social service work. She discussed moving away from "helping" and becoming a "meaningful advocate". In her critique of the technocratic enactment of social service roles, she discussed the importance of abandoning ideas of expertise to seek understanding of varied life contexts. She explained the need to understand intersecting societal factors that influence the agency of the people involved and honouring what they have been doing to navigate those oppressive factors:

> Rather than just jumping into a social work role, we need to deconstruct what it means to be in a helping profession. And if we can add one more word, we could move away from being helping professionals to being meaningful advocates. In my mind, social work assumes a level of expertise where someone who knows how to live life the best jumps in and tries to fix those who are having trouble without taking context into account. Advocating would involve listening to all dynamics at play, trying to understand the relationships involved, looking at the systemic factors that influence the situation (intersecting oppressions related to ethnicity, poverty, intergenerational trauma) and recognizing that everyone in the situation is probably doing the best they can with what they've got. Advocating involves helping those resiliencies become more important than the oppression. Working to meaningfully address the issues that people are facing, while taking into account the strategies and skills that they have for living in those situations. Privileging their knowledge.

Alison explained that, from her perspective, the idea of the "helping professional" needs to be deconstructed. She articulated the need to work as advocates rather than experts who help and to be vulnerable and submissive to those being served as experts of their own experience. In reconceptualizing "helping professional", she is re-signifying what social service work is and what it means to be someone working in that field. This is a response to dominant discourse that privileges the "helping professional" as an expert who works within a managerial culture, where they must demonstrate efficacy and efficiency to be recognized as viable subjects and to promote the continued funding of the programs within which they work. Alison's call for deconstructing helping professions involves those in the field recognizing how they are being constructed (through, for example, reporting requirements and funding) and the role of shifting power relations in re/constituting social service work. This resistance to neoliberal discourse and managerial or technocratic expectations is both risky and generative: while resistance to technocratic expectations may jeopardize recognition in neoliberal environments, it also provides the opportunity for workers to generate new ideals in social service work where they can be recognized as viable subjects in novel ways.

Performing Social Service Worker in Transition

Examining the social service worker identity as performance helps demonstrate the complexity of who a social service worker is and what it is they do. The concept of performativity clarifies that identity is not a stable characteristic but an ongoing performance and that the 'ideal social service worker' can be deconstructed and resignified. As seen, participants experienced the romanticized ideals of helping professionals as "selfless" and "passionate", who work to "save" those who are marginalized. Alison discussed how she experienced pressure from others (outside of social service) who wonder why social service workers are not doing their job and resolving inequalities, oppression, and issues like homelessness, drug use, and mental illness. From this perspective, the social service worker is an expert, exercising their power-knowledge by intervening in the life course of a 'client' to promote positive outcomes and resolve social problems. These outcomes, as discussed by the participants, are documented and shared to demonstrate effectiveness and secure ongoing funding. Participants like Alison, Hannah, and Carolyn discussed how this technocratic or managerial approach constrained their work, and they had to navigate ways to meet outcome-focused (i.e., funding) requirements while emphasizing the relational aspect of their work. They navigate contradictory pressures (i.e., technocratic requirements vs. relational practice) and are engaged in an ongoing process of subjectification in their performance as social service workers. They are living in a place of not-enough or in-between as they perform towards recognition. In seeking recognition, they may fall short and be relegated to precarity; in achieving recognition, they may regulate others to precarity. Achieving recognition reproduces and fortifies the ideal subject and thus, creates Others who fall outside of recognized subjectivity.

While a technocratic approach assumes that there are specific interventions that can be used to obtain certain outcomes with 'clients', the participants emphasized the element of uncertainty in social service work—not knowing what they were expected to do, what would be helpful to those they serve, or whether their work had a positive impact. Within the context of macro-level social problems (like violence, homelessness, poverty, and addiction), they asked, "what can we do?" They spoke of navigating uncertainty by emphasizing relational practice—by being present with others, by providing material necessities (a warm jacket, food, a safe place to stay), and by humbling oneself and not approaching the relationship as an expert. In relational practice, social service workers do not achieve mastery; the performance never achieves the ideal subject position. The subject position is not stable, and there are a multiplicity of social service worker subjects in various contexts. Instead of mastering a subject position, the participants recognized the importance of staying in a place of uncertainty—of being in-between or not-enough. Alison articulated the need to move away from the language of "helping professional". She argued for advocacy rather than helping, and in her push for re-signifying the helping professional, wanted to redefine the work. The approach she suggests makes boundaries between 'social service worker' and 'client' porous and flexible, redefining their relationship.

In social service work, honouring uncertainty is important. Social service workers are expected to be experts in their field, who have a professionalized identity and can demonstrate their effectiveness. The needs of people served are complex and require being present and open; working from this place of uncertainty takes courage. Especially when, as participants have noted, their effectiveness as social service workers is questioned. Social service workers' effectiveness is critiqued within the agencies they work for, as the agencies operate from a more technocratic approach and require reporting on pre-determined outcomes. Social service workers are even questioned by society more broadly, when they are asked why they have not resolved societal inequalities and injustice. It takes courage to recognize uncertainty as a strength and an asset, in an environment where the need for certainty is assumed and valued.

Social service workers navigate their relationships from this place of courage and uncertainty, being open to, and humble in the complexity of their encounters. Practically, this involves respecting and collaborating with those served and trying to diminish power differentials in the working relationship. Transition into the social service role is an ongoing performance of multiple identities, depending on the encounter. Working in a complex field with changing needs, knowledge, models, and funding is a continual transition.

Following Ideas of Ongoing Transition

Together, power and performativity offer important insights into the transition experiences of social service workers. Power flows through social service work and through the bodies of workers as they enact fluid, dynamic subjectivities throughout a continual transition. Social service workers can continually, in varied arrangements, re-signify their role in a way that fits for their understanding of ethical relational work as power flows and shifts and changes. Performativity builds on this understanding of power by deconstructing identity as fixed and stable and recognizing how social service workers engage in an ongoing performance of the idealized role of 'social service worker'. Social service workers perform this role within the constraints of what is recognized as 'good' practice; these social and cultural constraints shift across time and context and in relation with others. Transgressing these expectations, or performing outside of the ideal subject position, puts social service workers at risk for precarity. Recognition, as being enough as a 'good' social service worker, is thus relational and ongoing. These concepts allow for transition to be retheorized; transition does not involve taking on one identity, or transitioning from one identity (i.e., student) to another (i.e., social service worker). Instead, transition is an ongoing relational process. The next chapter explores this ongoing process through the narratives of the social service workers.

In the following chapter, I explore the phenomenon of transition as an ongoing process of *becoming* (Deleuze & Guattari, 2005). Transition is a dynamic process involving human and material agents, entangled in varied ways, each becoming at its own speed and direction. I explore the agential nature of some material elements discussed by the participants to demonstrate how social service workers, those they serve, the discourses they exist within, and the material environments they inhabit can create unique encounters. I explore how redefining transition as a process of becoming alters what can be made possible in social service work and education.

References

Butler, J. (1999). *Gender trouble: Feminism and the subversion of identity.* Routledge.

Butler, J. (2009). Performativity, precarity, and sexual politics. *AIBR - Revista de Antropología Iberoamericana, 4*(3), 321-336. doi: 10.11156/aibr.040303e

Davies, B. (2006). Subjectification: the relevance of Butler's analysis for education. *British Journal of the Sociology of Education, 27*(4), 425-438. doi: 10.1080/0142590600802907

Deleuze, G., & Guattari, F. (2005). *A thousand plateaus: Capitalism and schizophrenia.* (B. Massumi, Trans.). University of Minnesota Press. (Original work published 1980)

Jackson, A. Y. (2004). Performativity identified. *Qualitative Inquiry, 10*(5), 673-690. doi: 10.1177/1077800403257673

Jackson, A. Y., & Mazzei, L. A. (2012). *Thinking with theory in qualitative research: Viewing data across multiple perspectives.* Routledge.

Part 3

Re-Imagining Transition

Chapter 6

"We are Constantly Transitioning"— Transition as Becoming

The participants' narratives on navigating neoliberal expectations and learning to perform multiple subjectivities as social service workers demonstrate the processual nature of transition. The participants did not wake up one day with all of the knowledge and skills required for their complex (and often contradictory) roles and recognize that they had successfully transitioned from being students. Rather than transitioning from 'student' to 'social service worker', participants performed and continue to perform a multiplicity of subject positions; this demonstrates that the process of transition is an ongoing performance.

Much of the research on school-to-work transition assumes transition to be a linear and distinct stage; that is, students complete school and then transition into the workforce. Participant narratives highlighted that, among a number of other potential trajectories, students may work and attend school simultaneously, return to school for additional credentials, and/or experiment with various jobs before settling into a position. Ashton and Ashton (2016) found that a three-stage model of transition—education, transition, entry into work—was also insufficient for understanding the trajectories of dancers. While they recognize that many students take a more circuitous route to employment and/or work and attend school simultaneously, their work goes beyond this critique of the three-stage model. They explain that for their participants, "the various components of the transition, family, school and work are coterminous, they run together and there is no endpoint to the transition" (Ashton & Ashton, 2016, p. 749). Nairn et al. (2012) also found, in their longitudinal discussions with young people leaving school in New Zealand, that:

> ... This is a generation for whom, the linearity of consecutive life-stage transitions has been replaced by the complexity of concurrent transitions: transitions from the parental home to independence, from family of origin to other living situations, and from education to employment are neither as linear nor as unidirectional as they were for previous generations. (p. 38).

As participant narratives have highlighted how power works on and through them as they perform a multiplicity of social service worker identities, transition is not one distinct aspect. Rather than experiencing the transition from school to work, there are multiple transitions as social service workers continually navigate their role. Transition, then, is a complex, coterminous process with no end.

This conceptualization of transition as ongoing and relational foregrounds the human individual and their agency. That is, while performativity allows for dynamic identities, the concept focuses on individual human agency in the performance and construction of these identities. This humanist conceptualization of the subject is rejected by feminists (Braidotti, 2013), post-structuralists (St. Pierre, 2000), post-humanists (Barad, 2003) and other theorists. Critics of a humanist subject argue that the conceptualization of a stable individual, who holds and exercises agency, creates a binary of Self/Other, where the self is privileged and the other is seen as foreign and inferior and is, thus, disadvantaged (St. Pierre, 2000; Braidotti, 2013). These binaries include Man/Woman, Human/Nature, and Subject/ Object (St. Pierre, 2000); in each, the first enunciation is valued and the second exists only in relation to the first. To help deconstruct the human subject, Braidotti (2013) draws on the enlightenment ideal of Leonardo da Vinci's Vitruvian Man, as the icon of bodily perfection, rational progress and hegemonic cultural (i.e., European) ideals; she explains that this notion of the human subject is ethnocentric, raced, classed, patriarchal, heteronormative, and imperialist. Emphasizing the primacy of the human subject promotes binaries, hierarchies, and systems of classification that have real material effects on people's lives (St. Pierre, 2000).

Karen Barad, a feminist theorist and physicist, moves beyond the human subject in her articulation of post-humanist performativity. She states that a post-humanist performativity is:

> One that incorporates important material and discursive, social and scientific, human and non-human, and natural and cultural factors. A posthuman account calls into question the givenness of the differential categories of 'human' and 'nonhuman', examining the practices through which these differential boundaries are stabilized and destabilized. (Barad, 2003, p. 808)

This conceptualization blurs distinctions between human/ non-human, nature/culture, and material/discursive, recognizing how these are mutually constituted and inseparable. This blurring alters the traditional idea of the subject as a human who holds and exercises agency. Post-human performativity moves beyond the human, proposing fluidity between human and non-human agents and recognizing the inseparability of these elements. None of these elements is inherently more important or influential than another; the traditional hierarchical relationship is flattened.

To think through transition differently, I needed to examine social service workers as one integral element of the transition phenomenon. Depending on my articulation, this phenomenon includes other integral people and things in an entangled relationship. Moving from the individual to the entangled phenomenon as the unit of analysis allows me to explore more deeply the relationality of the people, things, space, and time that constitute social service work and transition.

In this chapter, I explore the concepts of *becoming* and *entanglement* that allow for a more nuanced understanding of transition as an ongoing, relational process. First, I explore the concept of *becoming* (Deleuze & Guattari, 2005)—a process of continual transition that shapes all living and non-living material. I put *becoming* to work to examine the transition from school to working in social services as a continual and ongoing process involving *entanglements* of human and non-human agents intra-acting (Barad, 2007). Rather than examining the development of an individual within an external context—in this case, new social service workers navigating their role— human agents are co-constituted in entanglements with other agents. These agents, or elements of the entanglement, intra-act rather than inter-act because they are intertwined and inseparable within the entanglement; they exist in relation to one another. Entanglements are dynamic, constantly forming and reforming—each element in the entanglement is in an ongoing process of becoming. The elements or agents intra-act and then move on into new entanglements, different than they were before the encounter. I draw on two examples from the participants' narratives—a jacket and a cup of tea—in an attempt to make these entanglements more visible and tangible and to explore the materiality of social service work.

Thinking through the concepts of entanglement and becoming allows for the transition to be viewed as a relational process of inseparable human and material agents, each of which is dynamic and evolving. This then shifts the focus from the individual participants and how they navigate transition, to how the participants are becoming 'social service workers'. How are they becoming with their 'clients'? Or with me in our research entanglement? How do these entanglements influence becoming? And most importantly, how do intra-actions in social service and educational entanglements provide potentiality for a more ethical, just world?

Becoming

Becoming is ongoing transition. It is an unfinalizable process involving the "replacement of static conceptions of things through the creation of dynamic conceptions of processes in continual transition" (Grosz, 2005, p. 10). This process of continual transition is not distinct to human life but involves all living and non-living elements:

> Becoming is thus not a capacity inherited by life, an evolutionary outcome or consequence, but is the very principle of matter itself, with its possibilities of linkage with the living, with its possibilities of mutual transformation, with its inherent and unstable volatility (Grosz, 2005, p. 10).

All matter is becoming; living and non-living elements are created as new possibilities in "mutual transformation" (Grosz, 2005, p. 10). Potentiality exists in becoming; what one was or what one became is not important. According to Deleuze and Guattari (2005),

> Becoming produces nothing other than itself. We fall into a false alternative if we say that you either imitate or you are. What is real is the becoming itself, the block of becoming, not the supposedly fixed terms through which that which becomes passes. (p. 238).

Deleuze and Guattari (2005) go on to explain that "a becoming is not a correspondence between relations. But neither is it a resemblance, an imitation, or, at the limit, an identification … To become is not to progress or regress along a series" (p. 237-238). In other words, becoming is not a series of steps towards an endpoint or a regression away from a finalized identification; it is not a path between two points. Becoming is not an attribute of an individual and it is not a linear process between a start point and an endpoint. Traditional transition models assume a linear and finalizable process involving a "student" transitioning to a "worker". The individual is responsible for navigating this process "successfully" by accessing supports and interventions as needed to reach the desired outcome of relevant work that is commensurate with one's credential.

Unlike three-stage models of transition (school–transition–work) that assume that an individual achieves a specific endpoint, becoming is an ongoing relational process. The individual—in a state of continual transition—is constituted in relation. I introduced this idea in Chapter 4 when examining how Alison feels like she has failed in her transition to being an adult when she compares her life to what she sees as societal expectations of where she should be in relation to education, employment, financial security, and other neoliberal measures of success. She noted that even when neoliberal values are incongruent with her own, it is difficult to stop and question whether those measures are important to her. Even when she determines those measures of success are incongruent with her own values or goals, she finds being viewed as unsuccessful by others (using neoliberal measures) has a negative impact on her sense of self:

> Even within my own values, none of this is important to me, but I make sense of myself also through how others see me. So, my identity isn't just internal—it is also relational. And if I am seen as not quite getting it right, it is going to have a negative effect on me.

Alison's discussion demonstrates the relational aspect of on-going transition. Recognizing transition as ongoing or continuous contrasts with perspectives that see the transition as a linear progression that can be successfully completed. Rather than seeing transition as a finish line that the student is responsible for passing, transition is part of becoming. Becoming is a constant transition—a continual process—with no start or endpoints. As Alison explains:

> We are constantly making meaning, *constantly transitioning*. In talking about transition, neoliberal ideas make me feel like I've failed to transition into being an adult. I'm 30. I've done a lot of pretty great things in my life. I'm proud of where I am. But I forget that all of the time. (Italics mine)

In her narrative, Alison recognizes that her transition is not complete; she is constantly transitioning. She is becoming. Unlike transition, as a distinct stage with a finalizable goal, becoming is being. The idea of constant transition—becoming—allows her to recognize that she has done a lot of important things in her life and feel proud of where she is.

Social service work involves multiple relational becomings within a field which is also dynamic and becoming. This shift in thinking emphasizes the ongoing nature of transition into and throughout social service practice. Not only are social service workers "constantly transitioning", but so are their "clients", colleagues, agencies, funding agents, conceptualizations of need areas (like addiction, mental health, homelessness), frameworks for delivering service, and other related aspects of social service work. It is within these entanglements that social service workers are constituted.

Entanglements

As introduced above, we (human and non-humans alike) are

constituted in entangled relations. We exist in intra-action with other agents. Entanglements are dynamic and shifting, and each element can be reconstituted into various entanglements, depending upon the enacted boundaries. As Barad (2007) discusses, what is made to matter is determined through a boundary-making process. Transition, as a phenomenon, exists as an entanglement of many inseparable parts: me, my participants, their experiences, our conversations, discourses that construct and constrain, workspaces, culture, and educational institutions. But each of those elements is more than they appear: human bodies, gender, ethnicity, memories, histories, brothers, sisters, children, parents, students, workers, teachers, courses, hope, grades, practicum, experiences, credentials, desks, hot coffee, stress, gratification, relationship, connection, support, clients, success, colleagues, funding agents, peanut butter toast, a good life, cartoons, a warm jacket, and on and on. These elements, and more, come into being in intra-action in transition.

In the phenomenon of transition, there are a multitude of entangled elements, including but not limited to: students, values, care, empathy, education, workers, labour markets, neoliberal institutions, classrooms, teachers, power, social service agencies and programs, meritocracy, financial ideals of success, hypercapitalism, violence, hunger, feeling "not enough", and precarity. These elements are inseparable and entangled in multiple ways. The phenomenon of transition is made of seemingly infinite combinations and arrangements of entanglements. For example, students studying to work in social services are also entangled in classrooms as physical structures (with artificial or natural light, chairs, tables, seating arrangements, laptops, connection, isolation) with deadlines, stress, pressure, discourses on what it means to be a 'good student', expectations of production (i.e., assignments, exams, and papers), attempting to balance employment and other responsibilities, in relationship with classmates, friends, family, instructors, and the wider community.

Making it "More Tangible"—A Jacket and a Cup of Tea

In explaining her approach to her work, Alison discussed the need to make things more tangible. She explains that working with young people with multiple vulnerabilities, who are constituted in very complex systems, can be overwhelming. I appreciated her desire to move from abstract ideas of social justice to tangible, material aspects of her practice, including making tea for the young people she works with. In keeping with Alison's idea, I hope to make the concept of post-human performativity a bit more tangible. To do so, I draw on Carolyn's discussion of a youth's jacket and Alison's example of making tea as social justice to highlight how human and non-human agents are entangled and inseparable. I use these two examples of social service work practice to explore how being a social service worker works.

My analysis involves re-storying the participants' narratives that focus on their experience and perspective; I shift the narrative away from a stable subject (i.e., a first-person narrative account) to highlight the material as integral and agential within the encounter and explore tensions and potentialities in how these material-discursive arrangements work. I then use the narratives to provide a tangible foundation for discussing the concepts of becoming and entanglement. Exploring transition as an entangled process of becoming-social service worker opens new imaginings in relation to "breath(ing) life into ever new possibilities for living justly" in social service work and education (Barad, 2007, p. x).

A jacket. Carolyn's discussion of the "harder moments" of social service work demanded my attention. In response to my question about what she liked about her job at a youth shelter during our first interview, Carolyn discussed that one of her favourite things about her job is what she termed the "harder moments". She explained that the youth who come into the shelter are often street entrenched (i.e., homeless) and may have addiction and/or mental health concerns. The shelter is not low-barrier (i.e., the young people must meet specific criteria to receive service), and young people at the shelter must be functioning well and working on their goals to maintain their placement. She discussed a harder moment that occurred when she met with a youth who had returned to the shelter after choosing to leave. He appeared intoxicated and returned to the shelter to ask for his jacket. Carolyn explained that she had brought him his jacket and sat down to talk with him. His vulnerability struck her as he explained how he was struggling with his addiction. He ran through a gambit of emotions—laughing, angry—while she listened with an empathetic ear. She noted she tries to show compassion because "life is really hard" and that listening to young people helps her understand their hardships, why they do what they do, and how hard it can be for them to make changes. Although the young person was no longer involved in the shelter program, it was a meaningful conversation for Carolyn; she said it provided a cause for reflection and makes her work worthwhile. It is a reminder to her that "behind every action is a lot of pain" and that everyone is just trying, despite being lonely and sad.

The jacket. This material element, and many others, become performative agents in this encounter. The jacket is not used by Carolyn intentionally in her work with the young person towards a specific end; instead, it is an integral and inseparable element, creating the encounter and constituting both Carolyn and the young person as worker/client. For a young person who lives on the street, the jacket provides warmth, a layer of protection from the elements, and a hood that shields the judgmental or pitying looks of people passing by. While the young person was feeling a variety of emotions–perhaps anger and disappointment for leaving the shelter, stress and anxiety about where to go next, shame in returning intoxicated to the program–the jacket was something he couldn't leave behind. The jacket drew the young person back to the program, where he, in his intoxicated state, could connect with Carolyn. In that encounter, Carolyn and the young person moved beyond their roles as 'social service worker' and 'client', and even beyond the boundaries defining them as separate people. In that moment, marked with fear, raw vulnerability, and uncertainty, Carolyn, the young person, his jacket, laughter, pain, compassion, understanding, and empathy are entangled in the program's physical space. Each in their own process of becoming, these elements intra-act to generate a new intensity.

Although Carolyn didn't discuss the physical space in which the encounter took place, I found myself imagining the space as I listened to her story. I can see an image of Carolyn and the young person sitting in chairs in a foyer space, an open area except for a staffed front counter. The walls are filled with flyers, posters for services, and art created by the young people who reside there. Young people (i.e., clients) and staff (i.e., social service workers) are moving in the space in different arrangements, in their own conversations; Carolyn and the youth have pulled rolling chairs, like what you find at a computer desk, off to one side, up against the wall, to talk. The jacket sits on his lap, and he methodically rubs the frayed cuff of one sleeve, as he speaks. This space, to the young person, may feel like safety, care, and connection. Returning to the program, to the physical space, constitutes him as a 'client', or as a previous (unsuccessful?) client who chose to leave the program. The staff on-site, including Carolyn, may have concerns about the young person being there in an intoxicated state – they may be worried about his safety or the safety of other youth who are in the program, they may be worried about his emotion-

113

al state and his potential to escalate. In performing their role as social service workers, they may view him as a possible problem—someone who no longer resides in the program who could trigger current clients or who could escalate and threaten the safety of the space. In their role, staff may attempt to keep him from interacting with current clients or try to move him out of the shelter as quickly as possible. While Carolyn may have thought of safety and the other youth in the program, they become engaged in conversation when she sits down with the young person with his jacket. Although it is emotional and challenging, they are entangled and inseparable; they intra-act with his story, pain, tears, fear, her anxiety, concern, powerlessness, the jacket, the hard chairs, the open drafty space. A true encounter.

A cup of tea. Alison also emphasized the significance of the material in her intra-actions with young people. In the excerpt below, she discussed how difficult it is to feel effective in her work, given social inequity and large-scale social issues. She recognized that making tea can be an act of social justice:

> I work through the problem on a case-by-case basis, in terms of where can I get a meal, and it makes it more tangible. School has a very grand focus on social justice, and it is humbling to recognize that making tea and checking in with someone while they watch cartoons is an act of social justice because no one else is checking in with them to see if they're okay. Recognizing that each youth is worthy of respect and dignity. I think it does make a difference. When I was younger, I wanted to be a social worker or a teacher, so I could "make a difference" or "change peoples' lives" and it is much less about that now. It is really just about seeing people and attending to them.

The act of making tea for someone becomes a way of being with them, of seeing them, attending to them, and honouring their humanity. Making tea and being with someone (e.g., sitting together on the sofa watching cartoons) shows the young person that they matter, deserve respect, and should-be treated with dignity. Making tea shows caring, nurturing, warmth, support. In hearing Alison discuss tea as social justice, I thought of warmth and safety. I thought of similar instances working with youth where the pain was so significant that nothing could help, yet we sat together and drank tea. I thought of, more recently, making tea in my office for students who were struggling, emotional, or wanted to sit and connect. I thought of tea ceremony, high tea, medicinal teas, and the importance of tea across culture, history, and geography. The tea—the making and offering of tea—becomes an integral part of the entanglement with young people. The tea performs within the entanglement, acting as an extension of the hand offering and of the hand receiving, so there are no boundaries between social service worker/client. In these encounters, I am drawn to the inseparability of human, material, discourse, and power within the entanglements. In these vital moments, the distinct elements of the entanglement are momentarily lost in true connection (intra-action). In these encounters, catalyzed by material agents, the inseparability of the entanglement becomes almost visible and tangible.

What is Possible in Thinking Transition Differently?

The shift from individual agency to dynamic entanglements opens different ways of understanding relationships and the complexity of lives. Thoughts, ideas, practice, discourse, and matter intra-act in entanglements, influencing what can be known and creating reality in each encounter. As Davies (2014) explains: "This idea of entanglement affects not just what is possible to see but *what is possible to be and do*, epistemologically, ontologically, and ethically." (p. 735, italics mine). If social service workers and those they work with, along with an infinite combination of other human and non-human agents, exist in entanglement, then these differentiated roles (i.e., 'worker', 'client') cease to exist. In entanglement, a social service worker is not separate from and superior (in terms of privilege, power, and expertise) to the person served. The entanglement alters what it is possible for social service workers to be: the social service worker is in a process of becoming-with the people they serve, and the other elements of the entanglement, as they co-constitute one another. This inseparability leads to a different ethical responsibility in social service work; there is an increased responsibility in seeing the 'client' as oneself. This alters what it is possible to know in terms of what relational work can look like and how relationality can be taught to future social service workers. Similar considerations can be made in relation to education and what educators can be and do, becoming-with students and other performative agents in learning encounters. I examine how thinking with entanglement alters what it is possible to do, see, and be in relation to social service work, educating social service workers and education more broadly, epistemologically, ontologically, and ethically.

Epistemological implications of entanglement. Thinking of transition as becoming in entanglement alters what we know and what we can know. The dominant understanding of transition—ascribed to by educational researchers, educators, students, social service workers, and most of the general public—involves students becoming workers (for a critique of this linear trajectory, see Ashton & Ashton, 2016; Nairn et al., 2012). There are, involved in this understanding, a number of assumptions about roles and boundaries. There is an assumption about professional roles and how work relates to identity. There are also identified power differentials between worker/client and educator/student roles and discussion on what the relationality between these roles should look like.

Thinking in entanglement erases these boundaries and roles and encourages us to examine relationality in a more fluid and emergent way.

In relation to social service work specifically, thinking in entanglement disrupts many of the foundational profession-alized bodies of knowledge that produce the field and have material effects for those involved. For example, theories of change, best practices, effective interventions, risks and protective factors, deficit discourses and pain stories (Tuck, 2009), and methods of diagnosis, classification, and patholo-gization shape social service work. These knowledge/power discourses determine subjectivity (as 'worker' or 'client'), constituting who is involved in the social service field and setting boundaries to their appropriate performance within the field. These discourses support and reproduce practices that are presumed to be inevitable. When we think in entanglement and eliminate the hierarchical arrangement and classification of worker/client, educator/student, human/non-human, and so on, the inevitability of these discourses becomes questionable. The assumed knowledge can be deconstructed, and new ways of engaging relationally become possible.

Ontological implications of entanglement. Thinking with entanglement de-centers the individual human agent. We exist in relation to. We are always becoming-with other elements of our varied entanglements. For example, the new social service workers who shared their stories and I co-existed in a research entanglement. In varied times and spaces, we became togeth-er, with a voice recorder, pages of narrative, hard chairs, and coffee shop soundtracks, and each element of the entangle-ment was made different in the intra-action. I did not exist as a researcher separate from the elements of the research entangle-ment just as the participants did not exist as participants—but together, entangled with a multitude of material agents (who are also becoming-with), we engaged in a process of mutual transformation. These participants are also entangled and be-coming-with those they serve in their social service work and the material and discursive arrangements that constitute them as 'worker' and 'client'. I am, as an educator, entangled with my students, the classroom, and dynamic agents (e.g., anxiety, desks, coffee cups, the smell of whiteboard markers, fluores-cent lights, pressure, laughter, due dates, semester, grades, and so on). It is the entanglement of these human and non-human agents that creates the learning encounter—this is an emergent process that is unpredictable and full of potential.

Why is this important? Well, it changes the way we look at everything. For my purposes here, it changes the way we explore school, work, and transition and creates new poten-tialities for more just and equitable approaches. In relation to school, understanding learning as an entangled process al-ters teachers' and students' individual roles and responsibil-ities. While constrained by (among numerous other things) curriculum, grading policies, and specific learning outcomes, a teacher cannot foresee how the teacher/students will become together. Teaching, in entanglement, recognizes how the stu-dents and the material arrangements produce different learn-ing encounters. One class of students will not be the same as another, nor will one class together be the same as the next. The learning process is emergent; each moment is different and cannot be replicated. From this perspective, school is an embodied experience of learning together in a classroom rath-er than transmitting information to achieve specific outcomes. All involved continue to become after the encounter but are different because of the intra-actions.

Very similarly, social service work is an emergent process of becoming-with. In relation to work, we are constantly tran-sitioning—always becoming-with those we work with and the discursive and material arrangements that situate us. Social service workers are shaped not just by the people they serve but also by colleagues, funding agents, the dynamic conceptualizations of relational work, and professionalized bodies of knowledge that we have explored above. They are becoming-with these elements in a field that is dynamic and becoming.

Reconceptualizing school and work as entangled experiences of becoming changes the way we view students, educators, and educators. Neoliberal conceptions of students (as commodities) emphasize individual factors that influence a student's ability to be successful. Thinking with entanglements alters our connection and responsibility to one another and to the world.

Ethical implications of entanglement. My responsibility goes beyond being an ethical educator, researcher, or practitioner; according to Barad (2007; 2010; 2012), responsibility is a condition of existence. She argues that we are "constituted in response-ability" (Barad, 2012, p. 215); meaning we have the ability "to respond, to be responsible, (and) to take responsibility for that which we inherit" (Barad, 2010, p. 264). I have a responsibility and a response-ability (an ability to respond ethically and responsibly) in my connection with others. For Barad, responsibility is not a choice but a condition of interdependence; being responsible is recognizing and honouring the "stranger threaded through oneself and through all being and non/being" (Barad, 2012, p. 217). As a critical scholar/practitioner, I have a responsibility and a response-ability to think differently. The purpose of thinking differently in research is to provide new potentialities to live differently—to live more justly. The goal of thinking unthought thoughts and imagining new ways of being is to address the injustices of our current situation. How can thinking differently help us live differently? As Barad (2007) explains:

The world and its possibilities for becoming are remade in each meeting. How then shall we understand our role in helping con-

stitute who and what come to matter? ... Mattering and its possibilities and impossibilities for justice are integral parts of the
universe in becoming; an invitation to live justly is written into
the very matter of being ... The yearning for justice, a yearning
larger than any individual or sets of individuals, is the driving
force behind this work, which is therefore necessarily about
our connections and responsibilities to one another—that is,
entanglements. (p. x-xi)

Barad emphasizes the importance of justice and creating new
potentials for justice by disrupting patterns of thinking and re-
making the world anew through connections and responsibilities to one another. Understanding that we are constructed and
remade in our connections creates possibility and hope. Specifically, rethinking transition can shed light on living justly
in relation to marginalized populations, helping professionals,
students, educators, and education more broadly. The risks
and responsibilities involved in living justly will be explored
in the next chapter.

References

Ashton, H. S., & Ashton, D. N. (2019). "Bring on the dancers": Reconceptualising the transition from school to work. *Journal of Education and Work, 29*(7), 747-766. doi:
10.1080/13639080.2015.1051520

Barad, K. (2003). Posthumanist performativity: Toward an understanding of how matter comes to
matter. *Signs: Journal of Women in Culture and Society, 28*(3), 801-831.

Barad, K. (2007). *Meeting the universe halfway: Quantum physics and the entanglement of matter and
meaning.* Duke University Press.

Braidotti, R. (2013). *The posthuman.* Polity Press.

Davies, B. (2014). Reading anger in early childhood intra-actions: A diffractive analysis. *Qualitative
Inquiry, 20*(6), 734-774. doi: 10.1177/1077800414530256

Grosz, E. (2005). Bergson, Deleuze and the becoming of unbecoming. *Parallax, 11*(2), 4-13. doi:
10.1080/13534640500058434

Nairn, K., Higgins, J., & Sligo, J. (2012). *Children of Rogernomics: A neoliberal generation leaves
school.* Otago University Press.

St. Pierre, E. A. (2000). Post-structural feminism in education: An overview. *International Journal of
Qualitative Studies in Education, 13*(5), 477-515. doi: 10.1080/09518390050156422

Tuck, E. (2009). Suspending damage: A letter to communities. *Harvard Educational Review, 79*(3),
409-427.

Chapter 7

Risks and Responsibilities

Examining social service workers' experiences of transition through the concepts of power and performativity helps deconstruct dominant narratives around students, school, transition, and work. Current transition literature is insufficient in understanding the unique experience of social service workers. This literature is built upon assumptions regarding education, work, and transition that do not capture the complexity of social service workers' experiences. To summarize, most transition literature accepts the dominant discourse of social mobility, assuming that education is a pathway to social and economic success. This idea–that hard work and educational attainment will lead to a good life–is sustained by neoliberal ideology that emphasizes individualism, responsibility, and competition. An assumption underlying much of the transition literature is that education and the labour market are meritocracies that reward individual agency and hard work and that 'success' can be measured by income or earning potential. Researchers examining transition seek to maximize 'successful' transitions through various interventions and supports based on these assumptions. However, as we see in our exploration of the transition experiences of social service workers, this dominant conceptualization of transition lacks complexity.

Social service workers are a unique group who face specific challenges in transition. Students studying to work with marginalized groups in the community are an "educational underclass", a group of primarily non-traditional students who study to enter a field marked by precarious employment (Deil-Amen & DeLuca, 2010). Social service work is tenuously funded, and workers face the significant challenge of engaging in very relational work with highly marginalized populations. There is a high risk of vicarious trauma and toxic stress (Cohen & Collens, 2013). Social service workers give themselves to the work but are under-resourced and overworked and asked to enact an ethics of care within a managerial environment. While social service workers offer themselves to the relational work with those they serve, they must also justify their work in increasingly neoliberal environments that operate under a business model.

Given that much of the existing transition literature does not speak to these unique experiences of social service workers, I examined the complexity of this transition from post-secondary to work. Specifically, I challenged social mobility discourse–fed by neoliberal ideologies protecting social efficiency needs–that education is a pathway to success by examining labour market realities and the precarity of social service work. This enabled the deconstruction of transition as an individual experience, where a student moves through a discrete and linear process to an endpoint where they identify and are recognized as a worker. The 'social service worker' is not one concrete and distinct identity but comprises multiple and dynamic subjectivities. Examining the participants' narratives through concepts of power, performativity, becoming, and entanglement, presented transition as a relational, dynamic, and ongoing process. As a new social service worker, one participant described herself as "in-between" and "still figuring it out"; this helps define transition as a state of always in-between and always figuring it out.

As they are always "figuring it out", participants do not discuss transition as a distinct stage that is completed and can be assessed as successful/unsuccessful. In fact, in recruiting participants, it became clear to me that defining a social service worker as new to the field was challenging. Despite experience working in helping roles, several participants felt new in their social service worker positions. Their narratives also included ideas of continual transition. This demonstrates that the period of transition is not distinct but can be ongoing, as the social service worker, the people they serve and their complex lives, the agencies in which they operate, and macro-level factors (like political climate, societal awareness and acceptance, and economic realities) are all dynamic and in constant transition—becoming.

As seen in the narratives, the participants question and critique neoliberal values and measures of success and the related promise that hard work will lead to a good life. Participants are aware, through their relational work with others and through their own experience, that being 'successful' is not the result of individual agency; people have varying degrees of unearned privilege that shape their range of options. As Carolyn discusses below, working with people with complex needs and abilities highlights how often the most basic measures of a good life are taken for granted by those who have them:

> I feel competitive but then I reflect on these thoughts and learn how to be grateful. Working in this field is incredibly humbling. People are dealt really shitty hands. And you forget to see how much you've been given. I get to eat three times a day. I have people who love me and I love people. Still, it is a very real struggle to remember, to be thankful, and to try to maintain balance. It is easy to slip into that competitive mindset without even being conscious of it.

The idea that "people are dealt really shitty hands" is not accounted for in neoliberal ideology. Carolyn's discussion not only highlights that people face varying (and often intersecting) degrees of disadvantage but also demonstrates her ability to critically resist neoliberal definitions of 'success'. Through their work with others and in navigating their own transitions, the participants recognize that being successful or having a 'good life' is not synonymous with wealth or material acquisitions. Rather, the definition of a 'good life' will vary based on values, abilities, beliefs, challenges, and experiences. Drawing on Carolyn's discussion above, for some leading a 'good life' may mean food security or building positive, loving connections. For those using social services, finding a warm, safe place to be, living independently, or accessing supports when needed may be significant aspects of having a good life.

As power flows through the various entanglements involved in the phenomenon of transition, there is always the potential for resistance. While subjectified through power relations, social service workers are not "restricted to the power through which (they) are shaped" (Honan et al., 2000, p. 23); that is, once recognized as viable subjects, the social service workers have access to a wider range of options than was initially afforded them. As Honan et al. (2000) explain, being constructed and recognized as a subject within power relations "does not mean that you cannot take up the power so achieved in gaining that recognizability to exceed, to go beyond what those who afforded you recognition had imagined possible" (p. 21-22). Examining the participants' experiences helps highlight that while social service workers are constructed in specific ways (i.e., power works on them), they are not limited to the construction that creates and recognizes them as subjects. As seen in the narratives, there are moments of resistance in transition, where transition can be retheorized, and social service work can be reconstructed.

As social service workers are always performing, there is always opportunity for resistance. In their state of "continual transition" (Grosz, 2005, p. 10), there are opportunities to resist dominant ideals of what it means to be a social service worker. One example of this is in navigating neoliberal values; even the act of stopping and questioning taken-for-granted values, discourses, beliefs, and practices provides a spark of potentiality. Although moments of resistance may be fleeting, these moments produce the possibility for change. In thinking transition differently, there is potentiality to respond differently, and to create the world anew. As demonstrated in the narratives, our response-ability, or ability to respond, involves being awake to opportunities to respond and recognizing our own ability to respond differently. Responding differently has meaningful, material implications for social service work practice, education, and work.

Social Service Work Practice

Thinking of social service workers as engaged in an ongoing process of becoming-with alters the role of social service workers and their relationships with those they serve. Social service workers perform a multiplicity of roles, navigating various entanglements, and do not need to enter professional relationships as experts. Removing the expectation of social service worker as expert flattens the hierarchical relationship that exists between 'professional' and 'client' and alters responsibility. In the traditional hierarchical relationship, the 'professional' is knowledgeable, accomplished and complete, and in this role, they hold power over the 'client'. The 'client' is viewed as lacking, flawed and fragmented, in need of expert help. As the expert, the social service worker is responsible for providing information and answers and the 'client' is subsequently responsible for internalizing this information

125

and enacting changes. When change isn't fast or substantial enough to be captured according to pre-determined outcome measures, blame falls on the 'client'. Rather than question the hierarchical relationship, the professional's approach, or the complex interaction of social, historical, economic, political, and institutional influences that may be constraining change, the motivation and commitment of the 'client' is questioned. Moving away from a hierarchical relationship, where the social service worker is the expert, helps diminish the tendency to blame those who have been, as Carolyn noted, "dealt really shitty hands."

Understanding the entangled nature of social service work practice alters the professional/client hierarchy. Rather than enter their professional relationships as experts, the narratives demonstrate how social service work practice involves not knowing—relational work involves being with, attending to, and working through things together. Several participants noted that it is difficult to know what works as this relational work defies traditional assessment and reporting. Their practice is an emergent and dynamic process of becoming-with.

Social service workers can work relationally, being critically aware of, and awake to, emergent possibilities. This could involve being aware of time and space and the influence of other material agents on their working relationships. It may also involve being intentional in their engagement with those they serve (and others) and being open to the unique humanity of each entanglement, rather than following a prescribed or technocratic approach. Social service workers can advocate for awareness of societal factors that promote disadvantage and suffering and encourage respect and connection for recipients of social services. This may involve resisting the hierarchies that impact both social service workers and those they serve. The humanity of recipients of social services is diminished when they are viewed as less valuable than citizens who are 'successful' by neoliberal standards. This puts them at real risk for dehumanization, suffering, violence, and death. The value of social service workers is also diminished as inferior to other professionalized fields that engage with people, for example, counsellors, psychiatrists, and social workers. As seen in the narratives of the participants, social service workers are critical, aware, intentional, and can resist what is to articulate what can be. Social service workers can also act as advocates in their agencies and to funding agents by encouraging humanity, respect, and meaningful resources for those they serve. Thinking/doing/being differently, as social service workers, has the potential to have real material impacts on the lives of those they serve. To actualize this potential, we—past, present, and future practitioners–need to deconstruct foundational aspects of social service work so we can move forward in responsible ways.

Many questions come to mind in critically examining social service work practice that require further investigation and exploration. What does it mean to 'help'? What assumptions are built into this idea, and how does this shape relationships? How might benevolent intentions unwittingly reproduce and reinforce oppressive power dynamics? How do dominant discourses in social service work privilege certain knowledges at the expense of others? How does working within these dominant discourses constitute those we work with in deficit-focused ways? How might we rethink the role of social service workers?

Education

Critical scholars have argued that despite teachers' best intentions and practices, education serves to reproduce oppression and inequality (e.g., Ellsworth, 1989; McLaren, 2007; Giroux, 2014, Apple, 2004). Kathryn Strom and Adrian Martin (2013) provide an interesting examination of this reproduction from a practitioner's perspective. They examine how neoliberal ideas of school, education, teaching, and learning can be operational within classrooms, such that teachers are reproducing these ideas, and the social inequalities they promote, without being aware of it. Other scholars agree that these dominant ideas may be unwittingly reproduced, even when teachers actively attempt to deconstruct and resist these ideas (e.g., Ellsworth, 1989; Cox et al., 2017).

Seeing teaching and learning as emerging out of intra-action could help disrupt neoliberal understandings of education. Much like the discussion of 'professionals' and 'clients' above, intra-active pedagogy could involve 'teacher' and 'students' existing on a flattened plane, entangled with other human and non-human entities as inseparable elements. I think teaching in intra-action would involve awareness of becoming and an openness to move and flow with the emergent ideas within the classroom. As a teacher, I go into each teaching/learning experience cognizant that the classroom experience and the enacted curriculum emerge through the intra-action of human (me, my students) and nonhuman (affective states, uncomfortable chairs, distraction, stress, classroom, the whir of an overhead projector, etc.) agents. I recognize that the material elements of the classroom (and beyond) construct our intra-action. I explicitly challenge the idea (with my students) that I am in charge of what happens within the class and that I can adequately plan my lessons to work through prescribed curriculum to meet specific learning outcomes. Rather than only working towards institutionally-defined learning outcomes for each course (which need to be standardized to similar courses at other institutions), I try to find new, thoughtful ways to explore learning; this exploration, for me, might involve be awake to learning in the moment (both mine and my students'), examining learning that happened in the past and can only be recognized retrospectively, and forecasting learning as it may happen in the future. I can teach my students about relational practice by examining entanglements, intra-action, and becoming. I can explore with them how those concepts can be taken up as social service workers and what taking them up may mean for them and for those they work with. I can explore concepts and ideas, opening new ways of thinking and new questions that can be asked, rather than presenting content as fact.

As educators, it is our responsibility to explore how, in our institutionalized roles, we may unwittingly reproduce neoliberal discourses and promote deficit-focused concepts of students that reproduce inequality. How are educators constituted and constrained within their role, and what tensions do they experience working within their post-secondary institution? How are neoliberal discourses filtered down through institutions, and how do educators experience these discourses? How are educators disrupting expectations of competition and traditional notions of 'success'? How might educators critically examine the complexity of relationships between school and work with students? How might educators explore ideas of meaningful or democratized work? How are educators' implicit conceptualizations of 'success' shaping their teaching/learning approaches? Are there tensions between student and educator ideals of success? How are educators critically engaging with curriculum to question and critique dominant knowledge systems? How do educators make space for varied knowledges and alternative discourses?

Work (and What it Means to Live a Good Life)

In North America, what you do (for work) is integrally connected to who you are, how others view you, how much respect you are afforded, and whether you are seen as successful. Think about meeting someone new, perhaps at a stodgy dinner party you really didn't want to go to. People will often ask, "So, what do you do?" as a shortcut to determining who you are as a person, and whether they want to invest further time talking with you. There is an assumption that our identity is comprised, to a large extent, of the work in which we engage.

The participant narratives have demonstrated that rather than having a fixed and stable identity, we each perform a multiplicity of identities. These performances differ in varied entanglements. Looking at work as a process of becoming-with, in entanglement, deconstructs the dominant assumption that who we are and what we do are the same (or at least have considerable overlap). Examining work as a process of becoming-with, rather than a final destination, allows for discussion of democratized work, and its role in living a good life.

Joe Kincheloe (1995) troubles the concept of *work* in a hypercapitalist society. Kincheloe (1995) conducts a Marxian analysis to argue that school and work are inseparable and that the current system of school-work increases disconnection (i.e., worker isolation, poor morale, increased bureaucracy, oppression, profit-maximization). Drawing also on Dewey, he examines modern efficiency and management strategies and their negative impact on democratic work arrangements. He discusses the social disintegration that has occurred as we have transitioned into a postmodern hyperreality. This postmodern hyperreality is marked by increases in unemployment and decreases in wages, such that workers cannot consume, which is the only remaining legitimizing aspect of labour (Kincheloe, 1995). Kincheloe further argues that democratic work moves beyond consumerism and consumption to meaning, belonging, ownership, and interconnectedness. His call is to democratize work to provide meaning and purpose, recognize all work skill levels as necessary and important, and promote respect for all workers. His vision of democratized work fulfills social efficiency needs while reconceptualizing what work means, as he imagines a system of meaningful work that is not founded on social hierarchy, inequality, competition, and the myth of meritocracy. His ideas raise important questions about how we conceptualize 'work'.

What makes for meaningful work? How can we advocate for democratized work? How does meaningful work fit within a good life? What are our responsibilities and response-abilities in engaging ethically in work? In the wider world?

Risks in Thinking/Doing/Being Differently

Intra-acting ethically in social service work, education, work, and beyond is transgressive. It works against the status quo of neoliberal discourse, which emphasizes individuality, personal responsibility, and competition. Recognizing the complexity of entanglement, becoming, and the potential for resistance is incongruent with accepting neoliberal ideology (and its material implications) as inevitable. In intra-action, our focus shifts from ourselves to being responsible for and intra-acting ethically with the human and non-human agents with which we are entangled. Rather than focus on our own success, relegating others to precarity in the process, we intra-act in a way that recognizes our inseparability.

Performing in a transgressive way against the status quo puts subjectivity at risk. If we are not performing towards the ideal, we are not recognized. Worse, we are relegated to precarity; we are not "recognizable, readable, or grievable" (Butler, 2009, p. xii and xiii). As Kuntz (2015) discusses, drawing on Foucault's concept of parrhesia (i.e., truth-telling), truth-telling necessarily involves putting one's membership in the community at risk. To speak and be heard as a truth-teller, one must be recognized as a citizen. However, speaking the truth puts one's recognition as a citizen at risk. Yet, despite this risk, the truth-teller speaks the truth to transform the relations of which they are a part (Kuntz, 2015, p. 118).

Social service workers and educators who emphasize ethical intra-active practice may risk expulsion from their community; if they transgress institutional norms and expectations, they may be segregated or face pressure from colleagues and supervisors to get back in line. Ultimately, if they do not adhere to institutional or organizational policies, they can lose their job. Social service work and education are increasingly marketized, with a focus on efficiency and effectiveness as demonstrated through predetermined outcomes; choosing to work outside of these neoliberal expectations can lead to precarity. As demonstrated by the narratives of the participants, it is increasingly necessary to navigate the tensions between ethical, relational practice, and technocratic requirements. Each of us, in our various roles, must balance our responsibility and response-ability with the risk in thinking, being, and doing differently. As everyone has unique circumstances with varying degrees of privilege, each individual has to determine the risks they are willing to take to transform the conditions in which we find ourselves. How can we work both within and against the structures that constitute and constrain us?

One drawback of complexifying the transition phenomenon is the incongruence of depth and nuance with prescriptive solutions or interventions. Unfortunately, with complex phenomena, there are no simple solutions. Rather than provide answers, I am hopeful that exploring the transition from post-secondary to work alongside other ideas, concepts, and experiences open the potential for new understandings. The implications of understanding how transition works–where how it works is an ongoing process and not a distinct state that can be understood–are that we, as social service workers, educators, and beyond, can engage in an ongoing process of working within and against how things are. Together, we can imagine a more just and equitable future.

References

Apple, M. (2004). *Ideology and curriculum* (3rd ed.). Routledge.

Butler, J. (2009). Performativity, precarity, and sexual politics. *AIBR - Revista de Antropología Iberoamericana, 4*(3), 321-336. doi: 10.11156/aibr.040303e

Cohen, K., & Collens, P. (2013). The impact of trauma work on trauma workers: A metasynthesis on vicarious trauma and vicarious posttraumatic growth. *Psychological Trauma: Theory, Research, Practice, and Policy, 5*(6), 570-580. doi: 10.1037/a0030388

Cox, R. D., Dougherty, M., Hampton, S., Neigel, C., & Nickel, K. (2017). Does this feel empowering? Using metissage to explore the effects of critical pedagogy. *International Journal of Critical Pedagogy, 8*(1), 33-57.

Deil-Amen, R., & DeLuca, S. (2010). The underserved third: How our educational structures populate an educational underclass. *Journal of Education for Students Placed at Risk, 15*, 27-50. doi: 10.1080/10824661003634948

Ellsworth, E. (1989). Why doesn't this feel empowering? Working through the repressive myths of critical pedagogy. *Harvard Educational Review, 59*(3), 297-324. doi: 10.17763/haer.59.3.058342114k266250

Giroux, H. (2014). *Neoliberalism's war on higher education.* Haymarket Books.

Grosz, E. (2005). Bergson, Deleuze and the becoming of unbecoming. *Parallax, 11*(2), 4-13. doi: 10.1080/13534640500058434

Honan, E., Knobel, M., Baker, C., & Davies, B. (2000). Producing possible Hannahs: Theory and the subject of research. *Qualitative Inquiry, 6*(1), 9-32.

Kincheloe, J. L. (1995). *Toil and trouble: Good work, smart workers, and the integration of academic and vocational education.* Peter Lang Publishing.

Kuntz, A. M. (2015). *The responsible methodologist: Inquiry, truth-telling, and social justice.* Left Coast Press.

McLaren, P. (2007). *Life in schools: An introduction to critical pedagogy in the foundations of education* (5th ed.). Pearson Education, Inc.

Strom, K. J., Martin, A. D. (2013). Putting philosophy to work in the classroom: Using rhizomatics to deterritorialize neoliberal thought and practice. *Studying Teacher Education, 9*(3), 219-235. doi: 10.1080/17425964.2013.830970

Appendix A

Methodological Approach

My Epistemology

To start, I position myself as a qualitative researcher and view qualitative research as a progressive way of creating new knowledge that challenges traditional modes of knowledge production (Denzin & Lincoln, 1994). I recognize that reality is created through our interactions with the world, as we are engaged in an ongoing process of meaning-making (Crotty, 1998). Knowledge creation is subjective, interpretive, relative, and partial. Therefore, research cannot be conducted in a neutral, objective fashion: the researcher is always part of the research (Denzin & Lincoln, 1998) and implicated in meaning-making. Qualitative research emphasizes uncovering subjective meaning-making through a collaborative, interactive, and respectful research process. One key strength of qualitative research is its potential to "make visible the politics and power relations of the everyday lived experience of the oppressed" (St. Pierre & Roulston, 2006, p. 678). Critical theorists also attend to the power dynamics involved in the research process and, while recognizing the power of the researcher cannot be abdicated, strive to create a collaborative and respectful research relationship with respondents that honours jointly constructed knowledge. The purpose of critical research is to end suffering in all its forms and emancipate all people (Kincheloe, 2008; Broido, 2002; LeCompte, 1994). It is the responsibility of an ethical, qualitative researcher to ensure their research serves a practical purpose and is meaningful to those involved in the analysis (LeCompte, 1994). I enacted this by grounding my research in an ethical imperative to create new understandings that could help promote a more just world. Specifically, I sought to eliminate the suffering endured by marginalized groups of people who receive social services. I intended for my work to demonstrate the urgent need to change the precarious material conditions both clients and social service workers live within. I believe that by thinking differently about our relationships with and responsibilities to one another, social service work and education can be made more just, relevant, and meaningful.

Critical narrative inquiry, as one qualitative research approach, recognizes that an individual's process of meaning-making is unique and dynamic; the identity of the narrator and their story is under ongoing development (Chase, 2005). As Clandinin (2013) explains, individual experience is contextualized within a complex life; narrative inquiry seeks to thoroughly explore experience within its wider context without essentializing the narrative. That is, the narrative of individual experience is explored within the social, cultural, political, historical, and institutional narratives in which it occurs; dialectically, macro-level narratives shape and influence individual experience as the individual constructs and affects macro-level narratives (Clandinin, 2013). A narrative inquiry approach recognizes that the narrator and the narrative are dynamic and continually developing, producing one another; through the process of reliving their narrative, the narrator learns about who they are (Clandinin, 2013; Hull & Zacher, 2007). An important aspect of narrative inquiry research is to determine how the narratives can disrupt hegemonic, oppressive processes and promote social justice and democracy; to examine, as Clandinin (2013) describes, how narratives "bump up" against existing narratives, creating tension and revealing new understandings. A narrative can be disruptive in its ability to demonstrate the social, cultural, historical, and political constraints that limit an individual's range of options for the construction of self and reality (Chase, 2005). A narrative can also promote social justice by highlighting the creativity and complexity of how people construct themselves within their world, despite these powerful constraints, pointing to new possibilities for living in the world.

From the start, my objective for using a narrative inquiry approach in my study was to allow participants to determine what is meaningful and relevant as they engaged in telling, re-living, and re-telling their narrative (Connolly & Clandinin, 1990) in a way that would promote critical awareness of their position and experiences. This approach is consistent with critical paradigms that seek to provide space for multiple subjectivities and voices (Kincheloe, 2008). It also recognizes that embedded within our own individual and social narratives, the participants and I co-construct meaning through a process of dialogue.

Narrative inquiry was congruent with my epistemology, my critical approach to inquiry, and my research question: how do new social service workers experience the transition from post-secondary education to working in the field? Encompassed within this question are three sub-questions:

- What tensions do transitioning students/workers experience? What narratives do they "bump up" against in their transition?
- How do they see, know and describe themselves as "students" and "workers," and how do they enact various identities across social, political and institutional

contexts? What shapes these identities?

- How do their personal narratives connect to socio-political relations?

Recruiting Participants

I recruited participants for my study through not-for-profit and non-governmental organizations that serve children, youth, adults and/or families who face various challenges (e.g., homelessness, addiction, mental health, unemployment, etc.). I emailed recruitment information to various agencies throughout the Greater Vancouver area. In contacting potential agencies from which to recruit, I tried to represent the diversity in the social services field; the contacted agencies differed in mandate/focus, philosophy, funding, organizational structure, and in their connection to other agencies. Recruitment was intentionally broad to elicit interest from new employees within social service agencies with a range of mandates; I hoped this would result in participants with varied educational trajectories, work experience, current employment, and transition experiences. I asked the agencies to post the information in an area accessible to employees and/or email the information to new employees.

Once I connected with participants, I also asked if they had colleagues, friends, or classmates who may also be suitable and interested in participating in my study; I sent recruitment information to each participant via email after our initial conversation, asking them to share the information with others who may be interested. I limited my participants to those who were "new to the field"; I initially defined this as participants who had been working in social services for less than one year (which is consistent with existing literature on newly qualified social workers). I found that defining a participant as "new to the field" was much more complex than originally conceived. Participants had travelled or done international work, had worked in various contexts but still considered themselves new to social services, had moved in and out of social service positions and other areas of employment, and had returned to postsecondary (while working in the field) for additional degrees. As social service work is diverse, so too are the experiences of those who work in the field, their role and responsibilities, and the degree of connection they have to the work. This nuanced nature of transition and the various trajectories I encountered in the recruitment process alerted me to the problematics of traditional conceptualizations of transition. I ultimately decided that participants were suitable if they considered themselves to be new to the field. All five potential participants who were interested in participating considered themselves new to social service work and, as such, were included in the scope of the study.

I did not sample participants to ensure generalizability to a broader population. The positivist foundations of sampling are incongruent with my critical, constructionist approach. A positivist critique of the participant group may highlight the need for more participants and question the homogeneity and lack of diversity within the participant group; this perspective assumes that there is a distinct range of possible experiences and perspectives related to a phenomenon and that perspectives may vary according to specific variables (e.g., gender, ethnicity, age, socio-economic status, etc.). Positivist research seeks to extract information related to all possible experiences and perspectives, thus the importance of reaching saturation and seeking out negative cases (Creswell & Creswell, 2018). From a constructionist approach, the range of experiences related to a phenomenon is unknowable (and possibly infinite); a sample cannot be defined that will represent all possible experiences. Instead, in determining participant involvement, I considered what matters in relation to the phenomenon of transition. I was interested in how narratives may differ in relation to academic trajectory, family and cultural influence, work and volunteer experience, current employment, and future goals. I recognized difference as potentially productive and generative. I considered how the narratives may be taken up beyond the individual experience in how they call attention to the discursive and material arrangements that affect the phenomenon of transition.

Interviewing

Prior to interviewing the five participants, I coordinated pilot interviews with three volunteers to test my interview protocol. I used semi-structured interviews to provide space for the participants to discuss the topics most salient to them. Unlike traditional interviews, where the researcher limits the topics for discussions to the information desired for the research (Weiss, 1994), in narrative inquiry, the researcher and participant engage in dialogue and collaboratively identify areas for discussion. The researcher may identify broad areas for exploration, but how the participants approach those topics, and what is important to them within those topics, shapes the narrative. I designed the interviews to explore participants' experiences relating to three interrelated topics: current employment, educational experience, and transition to work. The ordering of these topics was not fixed, and discussion of these topic areas differed by participant; that is, the participants shaped, through their own narrative, how these topic areas were discussed, what was emphasized or given priority, and what was most salient.

I met with five participants for a minimum of two interviews each. I recognized the dynamic nature of life stories and individual identities (Clandinin, 2013) and used multiple interviews as an opportunity for restorying. Our conversations occurred in public locations that were convenient for the participants and lasted one hour on average (ranging from approximately 45 minutes to 1 hour and 30 minutes). I audiotaped all interviews with participant consent. The interviews followed a general interview protocol, but I intentionally approached the interviews as conversations, opportunities for dialogue, where I would attend to and ask questions about the participants' experiences. I recognized that I was bringing myself and the narratives I am embedded within/construct to our conversation. I attempted to allow the participants to drive the conversation while recognizing that our interaction would shape our discussion. I was aware of, as much as is possible, the power relations inherent in our discussion and was intentional about attempting to build positive rapport with the participants; as mentioned, I wanted our conversation to evolve organically, and I did not want the participants to feel constrained in their discussion. I wanted to be open and patient with where the participant wanted to go and be actively engaged to pick up on threads of interest (Weiss, 1994). I was also acutely aware of what I was asking participants to do—reflect on and discuss their life experiences to someone they do not know. I suspected that our discussion may have been the first time the participants had reflected on what it means to be a student or a social service worker and how that may influence how they see themselves. Throughout our interviews, participants processed new ideas, thoughts, or feelings through our dialogue and figured out what they think about their experience by hearing themselves speak. Not only is it a challenge to "know" what your thoughts and feelings are related to an experience (e.g., transitioning from school to work), but it is also difficult to "translate" experiences. Devault (1999) notes that there may not be words or phrases that fit experiences, especially where the experience is gendered. She cautions to be attuned to dismissive terms like "you know" or "I can't explain it" as possible signs that translating the experience is difficult; these are places of tension, or difficulty in translation and these places may be very interesting (Devault, 1999).

All interviews began with a discussion of the participant's current employment; this often led naturally to discussions of their educational trajectory, how they came to be in that position, what they enjoy about their work and what they find challenging. Throughout our conversation, I consciously attended to the story and information provided, asking clarifying questions and commenting on the narrative in the moment. I chose not to take notes during the conversations as I felt this may be distracting for participants and myself (i.e., I may miss hearing elements of the narrative while attempting to write notes). Writing notes could have jeopardized our rapport as I could not fully attend to the narrative, and participants might feel apprehensive or anxious about what I was writing.

Analysis: Interim Research Texts

Clandinin (2013) states that interim research texts are created as a starting place of interpretation and provide space for the narrator (i.e., participant) and the narrative inquirer (i.e., researcher) to continue to co-construct meaning with the text. My interim research texts took two forms: reflective memos and draft narrative accounts.

Reflective memos. Reflective memos helped me remain cognizant of, and transparent about, my own narratives in which I am embedded. As the researcher, I made attempts to be cognizant of what I brought to the interaction with participants and how we were co-constructing our reality (Guba & Lincoln, 2005). To do this, I explicitly positioned myself and engaged in an active process of checking my subjectivities (Peshkin, 1988). The purpose of my reflective writing was not to improve my ability to interpret and represent data or to make my work more valid. I wasn't attempting to transcend my own subjectivity to access the truth in the narratives; this is what Pillow (2003) discusses as reflexivity as a methodological tool for improved rigour in qualitative work. Instead, my reflective writing served to question knowledge construction and how we, as unknowable, dynamic subjects, can know (Pillow, 2003).

Draft narrative accounts. I also created draft narrative accounts (as recommended by Connolly & Clandinin, 1990; Clandinin, 2013) to share my interpretations with participants. My descriptive interview notes (written immediately following each interview) allowed me to remember non-verbal elements of the conversation that could not be adequately captured on the audio recording. These descriptive notes provided context while listening and re-listening to my conversations with participants. I wrote draft narrative accounts directly from the audio recordings. These narrative accounts were then shared with the participant at the subsequent interview.

Unlike Clandinin (2013), I decided not to incorporate several interviews into one story or one telling. I saw the subsequent interviews as a form of restorying and recognized that each story can be retold in different ways depending upon time, place, audience, mood, experience, etc. (Mishler, 2004). To honour this and to represent each story as in progress and unfinalizable, I wrote a narrative account for each meeting rather than compiling the information into one coherent story. There is not one story that contributes to who someone is, but there is a multitude of stories (told by the individual and those around them, over time and space, to different audiences) that contribute to a plurality of identities (Mishler, 2004). Given the dynamic nature of our experience and our narratives, I did not want to impose new meaning on previously told stories; instead, I thought it was helpful to see the stories as a compilation that could allow for reflection and provide a transparent process of how we created (are creating) meaning in relationship with one another. The written documents are material artifacts that demonstrate the progression of our dialogue and meanings in the making. The narrative account for each meeting was shared with the participant at the next meeting. This narrative account then became the basis for our subsequent dialogue, allowing the participants to discuss elements in more detail, re-story, and respond to my engagement with our previous encounter.

Analysis: Thinking with Theory

Through the process of ongoing analysis, from the initial interview to the creation of interim research texts, I began thinking about the narratives through various theoretical frameworks (Jackson & Mazzei, 2012). I followed the affective intensities, the data that 'glowed' for me (MacLure, 2013). As I put theory to work in analyzing the narratives, I was led to new questions. For example, I found the concept of power helpful in examining how social service workers navigate the tensions between neoliberal expectations and an ethics of care. Power allowed for social service workers to both submit to and simultaneously resist neoliberal expectations in an ongoing process. As seen in Chapter Four, power was exerted on them in their role as social service workers and flowed through them as they found meaningful ways to work against these expectations. That examination led to a deeper analysis of pervading ideas of 'not enough'. The concept of performativity allowed me, in Chapter Five, to further explore the process of attempting to become the ideal social service worker, knowing that it is impossible to reach. The participants performed towards this ideal, reproducing it as natural and inevitable, while feeling it was a personal failure that they could not embody this ideal. The concept of performativity then led me to the idea of post-human performativity, where I began examining the entanglements of human and non-human agents. This allowed me, in Chapter Six, to explore the multitude of dynamic agents that intra-act in various encounters. Putting entanglement and becoming to work allowed me to examine transition as a complex, nuanced process involving much more than the social service workers themselves. This emergent analysis that led to deeper engagement with the narratives and the phenomenon of transition, also catalyzed, for me, different ways of thinking and being that have remained with me beyond the analysis of these stories.

References

Broido, E. M. (2002). Philosophical foundations and current theoretical perspectives in qualitative research. *Journal of College Student Development, 43*(4), 434-445.

Chase, S. E. (2005). Narrative inquiry: Multiple lenses, approaches, voices. In N. K. Denzin and Y. S. Lincoln (Eds.), *The Sage handbook of qualitative research* (3rd ed.) (pp. 651-679). SAGE Publications.

Clandinin, D. J. (2013). *Engaging in narrative inquiry.* Left Coast Press.

Connolly, F. M., & Clandinin, D. J. (1990). Stories of experience and narrative inquiry. *Educational Researcher, 19*(5), 2-14.

Creswell, J. W., & Creswell, J. D. (2018). *Research design: Qualitative, quantitative, and mixed methods approaches* (5th ed.). SAGE Publications.

Crotty, M. (1998). *The foundations of social research: Meaning and perspective in the research process.* SAGE Publications.

Denzin, N. K., & Lincoln, Y. S. (1994). Entering the field of qualitative research. In N. K. Denzin & Y. S. Lincoln (Eds.), *Handbook of qualitative research* (pp. 1-17). SAGE Publications.

Denzin, N. K., & Lincoln, Y. S. (1998). Introduction. In N. K. Denzin & Y. S. Lincoln (Eds.), *The landscape of qualitative research* (pp. 1-34). SAGE Publications.

Devault, M. (1999). *Liberating method: Feminism and social research.* Temple University Press.

Guba, E. G., & Lincoln, Y. S. (2005). Paradigmatic controversies, contradictions, and emerging confluences. In N. K. Denzin & Y. S. Lincoln (Eds.), *The Sage handbook of qualitative research* (3rd ed.) (pp. 191-215). SAGE Publications.

Hull, G., & Zacher, J. (2007). Enacting identities: An ethnography of a job training program. *International Journal of Theory and Research, 7*(1), 71-102. doi: 10.1080/15283480701319708

Jackson, A. Y., & Mazzei, L. A. (2012). *Thinking with theory in qualitative research: Viewing data across multiple perspectives.* Routledge.

Kincheloe, J. L. (2008). *Critical pedagogy* (2nd ed). Peter Lang Publishing.

LeCompte, M. D. (1994). Some notes on power, agenda, and voice: A researcher's personal evolution towards critical collaborative research. In P. L. McLaren & J. M. Giarelli (Eds.), *Critical theory and educational research* (pp. 91-112). State University of New York Press.

MacLure, M. (2013). Researching without representation: Language and materiality in post-qualitative methodology. *International Journal of Qualitative Studies in Education, 26*(6), 658-667. doi: 10.1080/09518398.2013.788755

Mishler, E. G. (2004). Historians of the self: Restorying lives, revising identities. *Research in Human Development, 1*(1-2), 101-121. doi: 10.1080/15427609.2004.9683331

Peshkin, A. (1988). In search of subjectivity – One's own. *Educational Researcher, 17*(7), 17-21.

Pillow, W. (2003). Confession, catharsis, or cure? Rethinking the uses of reflexivity as methodological power in qualitative research. *International Journal of Qualitative Studies in Education, 16*(2), 175-196. doi: 10.1080/0951839032000060635

St. Pierre, E.A., & Roulston, K. (2006). The state of qualitative inquiry: A contested science. *International Journal of Qualitative Studies in Education, 19*(6), 673-684. doi: 10.1080/09518390600976544

Weiss, R. (1994). *Learning from strangers.* The Free Press.

CPSIA information can be obtained
at www.ICGtesting.com
Printed in the USA
LVHW062137181122
733397LV00010B/116

9 781645 042563